Presented To
Cedar Mill Community Library

By the Ludke Foundation

Australia

Australia

By Jean F. Blashfield

Enchantment of the World™
Second Series

Children's Press®

An Imprint of Scholastic Inc.

New York   Toronto   London   Auckland   Sydney
Mexico City   New Delhi   Hong Kong
Danbury, Connecticut

Frontispiece: Sydney Opera House

Consultant: Tony Moore, PhD, Director of the National Centre for Australian Studies, Monash University

Please note: All statistics are as up-to-date as possible at the time of publication.

Book production by The Design Lab

Library of Congress Cataloging-in-Publication Data

Blashfield, Jean F.
  Australia/by Jean F. Blashfield.
      p. cm.—(Enchantment of the world. Second series)
  Includes bibliographical references and index.
  ISBN-13: 978-0-531-25308-3 (lib. bdg.)
  ISBN-10: 0-531-25308-2 (lib. bdg.)
  1. Australia—Juvenile literature. I. Title.
  DU96.B54 2012
  994—dc23   2011031121

Australia

Contents

Cover photo:
Sydney Opera
House

Eucalyptus tree

Kangaroo

Coming to Australia

SOMETIME BETWEEN FORTY THOUSAND AND SIXTY thousand years ago, humans came ashore on the land that is now the island of New Guinea. At that time, the ocean was shallower than it is today, and a bridge of dry land connected New Guinea to Australia. People could walk across that dry land to reach Australia. Over the course of thousands of years, many waves of people made the crossing.

Where did these first Australians come from? According to the stories told by some of these original people, called Aborigines by Europeans, they were created in the Dreaming. This was a time when ancestors and spirits lived together. Modern scientists, on the other hand, hold that many of Australia's first people came from the east coast of southern Africa. They migrated north up the coast and then east along southern Asia. Others may have come from Southeast Asia. The original Australians were probably the first humans to ever make boats that carried them across the open sea.

Gradually, these people multiplied and spread across the land. Groups that settled in different areas lived according to

Opposite: **Experts estimate that between 300,000 and 750,000 Aborigines and Torres Strait Islanders lived in Australia when Europeans began settling there in the eighteenth century.**

AUSTRALIA

- ● Cities of over 100,000 people
- ○ Other cities
- ✪ National capital

0   500 miles

0   500 kilometers

INDONESIA

PAPUA NEW GUINEA

Arafura Sea

EAST TIMOR

INDIAN OCEAN

Darwin

Kakadu National Park

Weipa

Coral Sea

Wyndham

Northern Territory

Daintree National Park

Cairns

Great Barrier Reef Marine Park

Derby

Purnululu National Park

Innisfail

Broome

Boodjamulla National Park

Townsville

Ayr

Port Hedland

Rudall River National Park

Tennant Creek

Mount Isa

Cloncurry

Bowen

Dampier

Karijini National Park

Queensland

Mackay

Exmouth

West MacDonnell National Park

Alice Springs

Winton

Rockhampton

Western Australia

Simpson Desert National Park

Carnarvon

Gibson Desert Nature Reserve

Gladstone

Uluru National Park

South Australia

Charleville

Maryborough

Meekatharra

Coober Pedy

Kalbarri

Lake Eyre

Sturt National Park

Brisbane

Geraldton

Kalgoorlie-Boulder

Nullarbor National Park

Gold Coast

Woomera

Lake Torrens

Bourke

Lismore

Perth

Merredin

Whyalla

Darling R.

Dubbo

Port Macquarie

Rockingham

Nuytsland Nature Reserve

Newcastle

Bunbury

Esperance

Gawler

New South Wales

Sydney

Walpole-Nornalup National Park

Albany

Adelaide

Canberra

Wollongong

INDIAN OCEAN

Mount Gambier

Victoria

Australian Capital Terr.

N

Geelong

Melbourne

W   E

S

Devonport

Launceston

Tasmania

Cradle Mountain-Lake St. Clair National Park

Hobart

Australia

the conditions they found there. Some hunted huge leaping kangaroos. Some fished on the edge of the sea. Some found ways to survive in the hot, dry lands in the middle of the continent. They developed different customs, beliefs, and cultures, as well as hundreds of different languages. Many indigenous, or native, nations developed across the continent.

A very different people arrived in Australia from a faraway land in the late 1700s. These people were from Great Britain, and they had their own way of looking at the world. The British wanted to acquire property and wealth. They looked

British explorer Captain James Cook first landed in Australia on April 29, 1770. He named the spot Botany Bay.

to the land for natural resources that they could use or sell. The indigenous people, on the other hand, did not think they could own the land. Rather, they said that the land owned them. The arrival of Europeans would drastically change the way the indigenous people lived.

European explorers at first just explored lightly at the edges of Australia. Then in 1788, officials in Great Britain began to send thousands and thousands of people to Australia. Many were convicted prisoners. Others were guards and officers to oversee the convicts. Most of the convicts had no idea where they were going. They just knew they would probably never see Britain again.

And so the British arrived on a new continent. While they called it their arrival, the indigenous people saw it as an invasion.

For generations, the newcomers mistreated or ignored the indigenous people. But the indigenous people did not disappear. Today, some still retain their traditional connection to the land. But all are now part of contemporary Australian

Making a Name

Long ago, before they had explored the entire globe, Europeans assumed that there must be a land in the south, if only to supply balance with Europe and Asia in the north. In Latin, they called it Terra Australis Incognita, meaning "unknown land in the south." By the 1600s, the name Terra Australis began to be condensed to Australia on maps. It wasn't until 1824 that the British officially accepted that name for the continent.

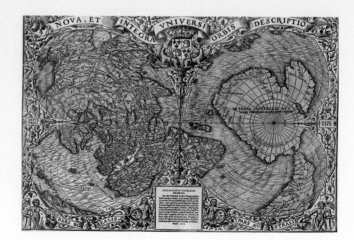

society. They use computers, wear the latest fashions, and eat food from supermarkets.

All Australians, regardless of their background, share an extraordinary land. In his book *In a Sunburned Country*, writer Bill Bryson describes it this way: "To Australians anything vaguely rural is 'the bush.' At some indeterminate point 'the bush' becomes 'the outback.' Push on for another two thousand miles or so and eventually you come to bush again, and then a city, and then the sea. And that's Australia."

That's a pretty good description of the landscape of Australia. It is a land that hosts a vibrant society that has influence around the globe.

Most indigenous people in Australia now live in the states of New South Wales and Queensland.

A Sunburnt Country

14

AUSTRALIA IS BOTH AN ISLAND AND A CONTINENT. What's the difference? An island is any body of land completely surrounded by water. A continent includes the continental shelf, which slopes downward toward the sea bottom. A number of islands around Australia are part of its continental shelf. Thus, Papua New Guinea, East Timor, and part of Indonesia are geologically part of Australia, which is the world's smallest continent.

The nation of Australia covers 2,973,952 square miles (7,702,500 square kilometers), which is almost as large as the continental United States (all the states except Alaska and Hawaii).

The Indian Ocean lies to the west and south of Australia. The Tasman and Coral Seas, arms of the Pacific Ocean, lie to the east. In the north, the Arafura Sea spreads out between Australia and Indonesia, while the narrow Torres Strait separates the Cape York Peninsula in northern Australia from Papua New Guinea. In the southeast, the island of Tasmania lies across the Bass Strait from the mainland.

Opposite: **Red crabs scurry across the shore on Christmas Island, a territory of Australia that lies in the Indian Ocean.**

Tasmania is one of Australia's six states. Victoria and New South Wales lie in the southeast, while Queensland is in the northeast. The state of Western Australia covers about the western third of the continent, and the state of South Australia is in the south-central part of the country. A region called the Northern Territory covers the north-central part of the country. Most Australians live in the eastern part of the continent, in the states of Queensland, New South Wales, and Victoria.

The city of Gold Coast hugs the shore in southern Queensland, a state known for its fabulous beaches.

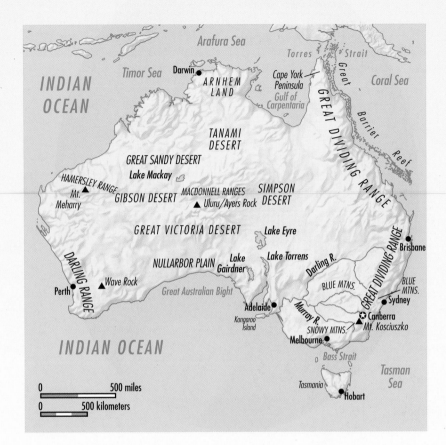

Australia's Geographic Features

Area: 2,973,952 square miles (7,702,500 sq km)

Coastline: 16,006.5 miles (25,760 km)

Highest Elevation: Mount Kosciuszko, 7,310 feet (2,228 m) above sea level

Lowest Elevation: Lake Eyre, 49 feet (15 m) below sea level

Longest Mountain Range: Great Dividing Range, 2,200 miles (3,540 km)

Largest Desert: Great Victoria, 163,900 square miles (424,500 sq km)

Longest River: Darling, 1,702 miles (2,739 km) long

Highest Temperature: 123.3°F (50.7°C) at Oodnadatta Airport, South Australia, on January 2, 1960

Lowest Temperature: −9.4°F (−23°C) at Kosciuszko Chalet, New South Wales, on June 29, 1994

Most Rainfall in One Day: 36 inches (91 cm) at Crohamhurst, Queensland, on February 3, 1893

William Charles Wentworth led the expedition that opened the grazing lands of New South Wales. He later became a powerful journalist and politician.

High Land

The first residents of the colony of Sydney on the southeastern coast were prevented from exploring westward by the Blue Mountains. These mountains are fairly low but are challenging because of their many gorges and canyons. Although countless generations of Aborigines and a few lone Europeans—probably runaway convicts—had crossed the mountains, it wasn't until 1813 that a European expedition made its way through them. William Charles Wentworth, one of the driving forces behind this expedition, was the son of a convict and would become a leading colonial politician. These explorers discovered abundant grasslands that were quickly opened up for farming and sheep grazing once a road was built.

The Blue Mountains are part of the Great Dividing Range, which is also called the Eastern Highlands. This 2,200-mile (3,540 km) system of mountains runs parallel to the eastern coast of the continent. Snowcapped Mount Kosciuszko, Australia's highest point, lies in this range.

Beyond the mountains is the Great Western Plateau. This dry, mostly flat region makes up the western two-thirds of Australia. On the coasts, the plateau has high elevations, but it drops down to low, flat land in the center of the continent. Australians refer to this vast, hot interior as the outback.

The highest point in Western Australia is Mount Meharry, which lies in the Hamersley Range. Karijini National Park also lies in this range, as do the nation's largest iron ore mines. A smaller range of hills in Western Australia called Bungle Bungles features colorful sandstone rock that has been carved into weird shapes by wind.

National Parks

Australia has more than five hundred national parks and several marine parks, including the Great Barrier Reef. Altogether, they make up one of the largest park systems in the world. Royal National Park, near Sydney, is one of the oldest national parks in the world, second only to Yellowstone National Park in the United States. The park protects coastal cliffs, long beaches, lush rain forests, and other landscapes.

A Sunburnt Country **19**

The MacDonnell Ranges are a series of parallel ridges and gorges in the Northern Territory. West MacDonnell National Park includes a spectacular walking trail that passes many indigenous rock art sites.

Deserts

Australia's largest desert, the Great Victoria Desert, spreads across 163,900 square miles (424,500 sq km) in Western and South Australia. A part of this desert is called the Nullarbor Plain. Nullarbor means "no trees" in Latin, and there are, in fact, zero trees in this region.

Treeless Nullarbor Plain stretches across part of southern Australia. It is about the size of the U.S. state of Nebraska.

The northern region of Western Australia is called the Kimberley. It was named after the Kimberley region in South Africa. They have similar landscapes, and diamonds have been mined in both places. South of the Kimberley is the Great Sandy Desert, Australia's second-largest desert. In the Great Sandy Desert, winds blow the sand into long dunes called ergs.

The Argyle Diamond Mine in the Kimberley produces more diamonds than any other mine in the world.

The Top End

Most of the Northern Territory is arid, but parts of the northern edge, called the Top End, are tropical and filled with lush plant life. The only city in the Top End is Darwin, the territorial capi-

The Rock Called Uluru

The largest single rock, or monolith, on earth is in the middle of Australia. Called Uluru or Ayers Rock, it is 1,142 feet (348 meters) high and 5.8 miles (9.3 km) around. It is located in Uluru-Kata Tjuta National Park, which is jointly managed by Anangu Aborigine people and the Australian government.

The Anangu consider it their responsibility to teach visitors about the land and keep them safe. They ask people not to climb the rock, because it is sacred to them and also because climbing on it is dangerous. Dozens of people have died while attempting to climb Uluru.

tal. From Darwin to Alice Springs, the only town of any size in the middle of the continent, is 800 miles (1,300 km).

Kakadu National Park, which lies on the coast in the Northern Territory, is jointly managed by its traditional owners, the Bininj/Mungguy, and by the national government. The park is filled with archaeological treasures, such as cave paintings and rock carvings. It is also home to a huge variety of animals, from crocodiles to kangaroos.

Australia's Island Territories

Australia controls several islands near the continent. Some of them are uninhabited, such as the Territory of Ashmore and Cartier Islands and the Coral Sea Islands. Heard Island and McDonald Islands are remote, tundra- and glacier-covered islands almost in Antarctica.

A Look at Australia's Cities

The capitals of the states, which are also their largest cities, are all near the coast. These cities and their suburbs are home to most Australians.

Sydney (below), in the state New South Wales, is Australia's oldest city, founded in 1788. Its population in 2011 was 4,596,328. Sydney Harbour, leading from the Pacific Ocean, features the beautiful Sydney Harbour Bridge, completed in 1932. The iconic Sydney Opera House, designed by Danish architect Jorn Utzon, has become a symbol of the country.

Melbourne, Victoria, has a population of 4,092,430. It is located on Bass Strait, overlooking the island of Tasmania. Old houses, electric trams, and big sporting and cultural events make this a historic and lively city.

Brisbane, Queensland (right), is a booming city of 2,056,290. Its skyscrapers, built along the curve of

the beautiful Brisbane River, house some of the nation's major businesses. Ferries and bridges are a part of the regular transportation system.

Adelaide, South Australia, is located at the mouth of the Murray River at the eastern end of the Great Australian Bight. Its population of 1,206,899 lives mostly in a densely populated city surrounded by many parks.

Perth, Western Australia, is located on the Swan River by the Indian Ocean. It is home to 1,554,769 people. Perth is the wealthy, energetic heart of Australia's mining boom.

Hobart, Tasmania, is Australia's second-oldest city and home to about 209,000 people. Nearby Mount Wellington, which sometimes has snow, is visible throughout the city.

A sign at the Christmas Island Airport welcomes visitors in English, Chinese, and Indonesian.

Christmas Island lies south of Indonesia. Much of the island, which has steep cliffs on most sides, is a national park. Most people who live there are of Chinese descent.

Norfolk Island Territory, located between the mainland and New Zealand, is made up of Norfolk Island and two other neighboring islands. In the 1820s, the British set it up as a place to send the most dangerous convicts.

Cocos Island is officially called Territory of the Cocos (Keeling) Islands. Two of these coral islands, located between Australia and Sri Lanka, are inhabited. One C-shaped island, North Keeling, and the sea around it make up Pulu Keeling National Park, where breeding birds and turtles are protected.

Water

The primary freshwater source in the interior of the country is the Great Artesian Basin. It lies beneath almost one-fourth of Australia and is the largest known aquifer, or body of underground water, in the world. In some places the water lies 10,000 feet (3,000 m) below the surface. The many stations, or ranches, on the land above obtain their water by bore holes (wells) that have been drilled down to the water. Until the basin was discovered in 1878, little land away from the coast was used for farming or ranching.

Finding Water in the Desert

Aborigines living in different parts of the continent learned where to find water. This knowledge was passed down from generation to generation over thousands of years. Aborigines in some places could get water from the roots of the red mallee tree. Other trees capture and hold water in holes in their trunks. Certain frogs naturally hold lots of water. Such sources as these meant that even people living in deserts had plentiful water. They stored water in bags made of kangaroo hide or large leaves so they would have water when they were in places with no water supply.

The Christmas Cyclone

Cyclone Tracy hit Darwin on Christmas Eve of 1974. It killed seventy-one people and almost wiped away the town. About thirty thousand people were left homeless. Darwin was rebuilt, partly with funds from a song, "Santa Never Made It into Darwin," by Bill Cate.

Many rivers labeled on maps of Australia don't exist except as dry riverbeds. Yet these rivers can spring to life in heavy rains.

The Murray-Darling river system generally has water, though not a lot. It drains a large portion of the eastern part of Australia. It starts as the Murray River, which flows from the Snowy Mountains of Queensland about 2,097 miles (3,375 km) into the Great Australia Bight, a large bay off southern Australia. The Darling River joins it at Wentworth in New South Wales. It became clear during a long drought in the early 2000s that the Murray-Darling system might increasingly dry up. The government is negotiating with farmers upstream to use less water for irrigation.

After heavy rains, Lake Eyre, in central Australia, becomes the largest lake in the nation. But during dry spells, much of the water evaporates and only a few smaller lakes remain. The dry bed of Lake Eyre is the lowest spot in Australia, at 49 feet (15 m) below sea level.

Climate

A land as big as Australia features all sorts of weather and climates. People along the southern coast generally experience four seasons. Northern Australia, though, really has only two—wet and dry. The Aboriginal people there recognize six, depending on what plants are growing and when the wind blows. In general throughout Australia, summer (November through March) is warm to hot. Inland temperatures may reach above 100 degrees Fahrenheit (38 degrees Celsius). Winters are cold in the south but warm in the north. The higher elevations in the south sometimes get snow.

Australia gets less precipitation than any other continent except Antarctica. Its desert areas are far larger than the rain

In the winter, snow often falls on Mount Macedon, near Melbourne, but it does not stay on the ground long.

forests that occupy its edges. Rainfall varies from 158 inches (401 cm) in the mountains of northeastern Queensland to less than 4 inches (10 cm) in the Northern Territory. More than three-fifths of the continent averages only about 12 inches (30 centimeters) of rain each year. The north gets winds and rains in summer, which is also cyclone (hurricane) season. That period is often called the Wet. The south gets most of its rain from May to September.

Australia suffered severe drought between 2001 and 2009. In February 2009, fires were started that burned in Victoria for thirty-five days. Whole towns were wiped out, and at least 173 people died. More than a million animals may have died.

Everyone thought that things would surely improve when the rains came. Unfortunately, they came too heavily. Places that had suffered drought were flooded in 2010 and 2011.

More than twenty thousand homes were flooded in Brisbane, the capital of Queensland.

Australians have learned to expect extreme weather. Poet Dorothea Mackellar wrote about life in Australia, about the land and the weather. She spoke for many Australians in her 1904 poem "My Country," which includes the lines:

I love a sunburnt country,
A land of sweeping plains,
Of ragged mountain ranges,
Of droughts and flooding rains.
I love her far horizons,
I love her jewel-sea,
Her beauty and her terror—
The wide brown land for me!

In her poems, Dorothea Mackellar memorialized the Australian landscape and the people who live in the bush.

Weird and Wonderful

IF YOU SEE A PICTURE OF A KANGAROO OR A KOALA, you think of Australia. It is the only place such mammals live in the wild. Koalas and kangaroos are marsupials. Marsupials give birth to exceedingly tiny and undeveloped young. The young spend many months inside a pouch on the outside of the mother's body, attached to a milk gland. A few marsupials, such as the opossum of North America, live on other continents, but marsupials are far more common in Australia. About 70 percent of all the marsupial species in the world live in Australia and nearby islands.

Opposite: **In 2010, Australia was home to about twenty-five million kangaroos. In wet years, there are more kangaroos, and in dry years there are fewer.**

Many Marsupials

Kangaroos have very large back feet with strong muscles that enable them to hop. Their front limbs are small. If startled, kangaroos stand up and hop in huge leaps, sometimes 6 feet (1.8 m) high and 29 feet (9 m) long.

The largest type of kangaroo is the red kangaroo. Male red kangaroos may reach 6.5 feet (2 m) in height and weigh 200 pounds (90 kilograms). These kangaroos occupy much of the

A young wallaby nestles in its mother's pouch. Wallabies usually stay in the pouch for about two months.

arid and semiarid middle of Australia. This same land is occupied by large cattle and sheep stations, so kangaroos are often shot when they begin to bother livestock.

Eastern and western gray kangaroos are slightly smaller than red kangaroos. In all, there are more than fifty smaller types of kangaroos and similar creatures called wallabies. One of the smallest is the musky-rat kangaroo, which looks like a small opossum. It lives in the wet tropics of the north.

One of the rarest kangaroo species is the tree kangaroo. The few that remain live in the forested areas of Daintree National Park of Queensland. Tree kangaroos are furry and look a bit like long-tailed bears. They are agile in trees and can leap from one tree to another. They are becoming endangered because their habitat is disappearing.

Koalas are small, furry creatures that weigh only 12 to 25 pounds (5 to 11 kg). These tree-dwelling animals have two opposable thumbs on each paw (humans have one on each hand). Opposable thumbs help koalas grab branches. The thumbs prevent a koala from falling while it sleeps in trees. The animals live in eucalyptus trees and eat its leaves, and those trees grow best in the areas where humans are expanding farming and creating other developments. Experts estimate that as few as fifty thousand koalas may be left in the wild, a drop of 80 percent since 1990.

Other Australian marsupials include the gentle, burrowing wombat. The smaller numbat, or banded anteater, of Western Australia eats mainly termites.

Fantastic Fossils

Riversleigh, in Lawn Hill National Park in Queensland, is a huge fossil deposit where the remains of living things settled for twenty-five million years. Many fantastic creatures lived in the ancient rain forest. There were marsupials similar to lions, and others the size of rhinoceroses. Some birds weighed more than 800 pounds (360 kg). Scientists have even found fossils of a crocodile that climbed trees.

The Tasmanian devil is one of the few marsupials that eat meat. These creatures, which live in Tasmania and are almost extinct, are very tough fighters and have powerful bites.

Other Mammals

Two of the world's most ancient mammals are found in Australia. They are the duck-billed platypus and the echidna, or spiny anteater. These animals are part of a group called monotremes, which are mammals that have features in common with reptiles. Monotremes lay eggs rather than giving

Platypuses have the bill of a duck, the tail of a beaver, and the body of an otter. They live in rivers and lakes in eastern Australia.

birth to live young as mammals typically do. They are considered mammals because they are warm-blooded and produce milk for their young.

There are only a few large mammals in Australia that are not marsupials. One is the dingo, a wild dog that was probably brought to Australia by the first people in Australia. Most dingoes live in the outback.

Other mammals were brought by later settlers and allowed to spread. One of the biggest dangers to small marsupials is the huge number of wild, or feral, cats. Australia has had feral cats since some jumped ship in the early days of British settlement. Foxes were introduced long ago so the British settlers could enjoy the sport of fox hunting. Both cats and foxes feed on wallabies, smaller mammals, and birds.

Dingoes are hunters. They eat animals such as kangaroos, wallabies, rabbits, and possums.

Termite Towers

A feature of the Australian landscape is the strangely shaped rocky mounds created by termites, or white ants. The insects build the mounds to regulate the moisture and temperature in their underground tunnels. Some termite mounds in Australia are 20 feet (6 m) high.

Camels were brought to Australia to help explore the vast deserts and build railroads. After the projects were finished, the camels were turned loose. As many as 1.2 million dromedary (one-humped) camels now roam the wilds of Australia. They are the world's only population of wild camels.

Beautiful Birds

Two animals appear on Australia's coat of arms. One is the kangaroo, and the other is the flightless bird called the emu. It is the second-largest bird in the world, trailing only the ostrich of Africa. Emus are common throughout Australia. They eat whatever they can find and can go for long periods without food. They have long, strong legs, with a cutting nail on the toes.

Another flightless bird, the cassowary, is found in northeastern Australia. It is a heavy black bird with a bright blue head and long red wattles hanging from its neck. Its head has a large fanlike horny structure called a casque. The Queensland cassowary is close to extinction because its habitat is disappearing.

With its long coastal areas, forests, and other habitats, Australia is home to as many as eight hundred species of flying birds. Many of them are colorful, including lorikeets, parrots, and the spectacular sulphur-crested cockatoo. Birds such as pelicans, gannets, albatrosses, and storks swim the coastal waters. A familiar sight along the rivers and wetlands is the black swan. These large birds with an S-shaped neck migrate through large areas searching for water. The laughing kookaburra lives in eastern Australia, where its famous laughing sound echoes through open woodlands and towns.

Cassowaries are among the world's largest birds. They live deep in the rain forest where they eat mostly fruit.

Although much of Australia is dry, it is not a barren continent. There is a reason that a lot of it is called the bush. Although that term is often used for anything outside of cities, it more specifically refers to land covered with low-growing trees and shrubs. The continent also has pockets of thick forests and wetlands.

At least six hundred species of eucalyptus, or gum trees, occupy the various terrains across Australia. Some are among the tallest trees in the world, almost as tall as California redwoods. Eucalyptus shrubs or small trees that grow in the bush are called mallee. They contain a flammable oil, which burns easily. If a

Hundreds of species of eucalyptus trees grow in Australia. Only fifteen grow naturally in areas outside of Australia.

The Great Barrier Reef

One of the top natural wonders of the world is the Great Barrier Reef. It lies in the shallow ocean off the Queensland coast in the Coral Sea. A coral reef is a deposit of the shells of the tiny sea animals called coral polyps. When the polyps die, their shells become cemented together to form coral reef. The reef serves as a home for many other creatures, including fish, sea anemones, clams, and sponges.

The Great Barrier Reef is the largest reef system in the world, stretching for about 1,600 miles (2,600 km). The reef is made up of at least six hundred islands and perhaps three thousand separate reefs. The reef system produces an estimated $5 billion a year in tourism.

fire gets started, nearby gum trees can explode, spreading the fire. The red tingle tree is a type of eucalyptus that withstands fires. In Walpole-Normalup National Park in Western Australia, a boardwalk built 131 feet (40 m) aboveground among tingle trees gives visitors a bird's-eye view across the forest.

Golden wattle, small trees with yellow blossoms, are often found beneath eucalyptus trees. A type of acacia, the golden wattle is the floral emblem of Australia and gave the country its national colors: gold and green.

It's estimated that more than twenty-eight thousand species of plants have been introduced into Australia. Many of them have spread wildly and taken the place of native plants. Prickly pear cactus was brought in as sheep feed and quickly spread. Blackberries, too, have taken over thousands of square miles of land.

Life in the Sea

Australia boasts many marine parks that protect the coasts and underwater marine life. In many of these places, sea life is incredibly abundant. In one location off Ninety Mile Beach in Gippsland, Victoria, 860 species of shore animals were discovered in about 100 square feet (about 10 sq m) of water.

Danger!

Some of the most poisonous animals in the world are found in Australia. The box jellyfish is so poisonous that brushing against one in the water can be deadly. These pale blue, transparent creatures are found mainly in the waters off northern Australia. Beaches there cannot safely be used in summer and autumn.

Another dangerous water animal is the blue-ringed octopus, a small octopus that lives in tide pools along southern Australia. It is among the world's most venomous marine animals. Although it is typically peaceful, if agitated it can bite, and its bite can kill. Great white sharks and tiger sharks are also a threat in the waters off Australia.

Many types of sea snakes, some of which are extremely poisonous, occupy the waters off the northern coast. Land snakes include pythons, which crush their prey to death.

Residents of the Sydney area have to watch out for the deadly funnel-web spider—or they did until an antidote to its poison was developed in the 1980s. These dark, hairy spiders that grow up to 2 inches (5 cm) across can be found in urban garages and yards.

Cane toads are not native to Australia. They originally came from Central and South America and were introduced from Hawaii into Queensland in 1935 to control the cane beetle, which was destroying crops. Since then, they have spread through much of the northern part of the country. They are endangering other species, because of their sheer numbers and because of the diseases and poisons they carry.

In 1935, 102 cane toads were released in Queensland. They quickly multiplied, and today there are more than 200 million in Australia.

The Story of Australia

P EOPLE FIRST SETTLED IN AUSTRALIA BETWEEN FORTY thousand and sixty thousand years ago. They spread across the continent. Different groups lived in specific areas, and their ways of life were related to the land and climate of that region. No indigenous group was very large. When Europeans first arrived in Australia, there were perhaps three hundred thousand people divided into five hundred different groups, or nations, each with its own language, beliefs, and ways of life.

The indigenous people of Australia did not practice agriculture as understood by Europeans at the time. Instead, they were nomads who roamed through their territories harvesting nature they knew well. They lived off a bounty of plants and game such as fish, shellfish, kangaroos, reptiles, and insects. Along the coasts, they ate mammals, birds, and reptiles, while in the forests, their food consisted of mammals, birds, and fruits. In the desert regions, they found a surprising variety of plants and animals. Although they had not invented the bow

Opposite: **Kangaroos were an important food source for many indigenous Australians.**

This Aboriginal rock art is near Alice Springs in the Northern Territory.

and arrow, they had an impressive armory of spears, nets for fishing, and boomerangs. But their main weapon was patience in tracking animals until just the right moment, which came from intimate knowledge of their prey.

Australia's indigenous people had no written history. Instead, they passed on stories and history by singing. They also passed on important information visually, in art. Some of this art can still be seen on rocks in the outback.

European Exploration

Probably the first Europeans to see Australia were Portuguese sailors in the sixteenth century. The Dutch stopped along the west coast regularly, to get water and explore. In 1606, a Dutch sailor named Willem Jansz entered the Torres Strait and named part of Cape York Peninsula. He is likely the first European to set foot in Australia. Another Dutchman, Dirk Hartog, came ashore on an island in Western Australia in 1616, nailed a metal plate to a post, and continued north. In 1642, Abel Tasman led an expedition that sailed around the southern coast of the continent to the island now called Tasmania in his honor. Tasman, however, called it Van Diemen's Land, for a Dutch East Indies official. Tasman sent a sailor to swim ashore to plant a flag, for the first time claiming the land in the name of a European power.

A statue of Abel Tasman in Hobart, Tasmania. Van Diemen's land was renamed Tasmania in 1856.

It was more than a hundred years later that British explorer Captain James Cook, sailing on a scientific voyage of discovery in 1700, defined the continent of Australia more thoroughly by mapping the east coast. He claimed the land he named New South Wales for George III and Britain. Cook did not understand the indigenous peoples' close relationship to the land on which they lived. Like most Europeans of his

Captain James Cook claimed eastern Australia for Britain in 1770.

time, he considered the land unused. He thought it belonged to no one and was up for grabs. At the time, European powers were competing for colonies. Australia became part of the British Empire, which was a military and trade superpower that had colonies around the globe.

Colonizing the Continent

At one time, more than 220 crimes were punishable by death in Britain. In time, British officials eventually decided that was too harsh, but they didn't have enough prisons to house all the convicts they didn't hang. Their solution was to transport prisoners to the colonies, especially to the American colonies, for crimes as small as stealing a loaf of bread. After the American Revolution, when the United States gained its independence from Britain, convicts could no longer be sent there.

Instead, prisoners were packed onto old ships called hulks, which were moored in British rivers. At that time in Britain, people were pouring out of the countryside into the rapidly growing cities to look for work. If they couldn't find work, some turned to crime to survive. In response, Britain passed harsh laws to protect property. This led to a huge growth in the number of convicts. The hulks were not able to house them all.

British leaders turned toward Australia for a solution to their convict problem. In 1788, the government sent a fleet of ships under the command of Captain Arthur Phillip, to build the colony of New South Wales as a penal colony. This prison colony would become known as Botany Bay, Captain Cook's name for the Sydney port where he had landed.

The First Fleet carried 778 convicts to Botany Bay.

Eleven ships making up what is known as the First Fleet carried prisoners, government officials, and troops to establish the colony. The British ignored the fact that there were already people living there.

The First Fleet arrived at Botany Bay on January 19 and 20, 1788. They then moved to a better location at Port Jackson, where the Parramatta River empties into the sea. Today, this is Sydney Harbour. There, they started the first settlement on

January 26. This date is now celebrated as Australia Day and mourned by many indigenous Australians as Invasion Day.

The British government had not planned well. There was neither enough food on the ships nor enough experienced farmers to grow food. Many of the first settlers—both convicts and government workers—died. A second fleet was sent, but many died on the long voyage, and those who survived could do little to help the first settlers.

Gradually, though, the surviving settlers began to grow food and graze animals to survive. Over time, other penal colonies were created, and eventually most of today's states of Australia were established as colonies.

Convicts were first sent to Van Diemen's Land in 1803. Their settlement became the city of Hobart. That same year, the British noticed that the French might be eyeing the southeastern corner of the continent. They started a new settlement in that area, which became the state of Victoria. The

Who Owns the Land?

The British claimed they had the right to settle Australia because of an ancient legal idea called *terra nullius*, meaning "no man's land." Under this idea, the British claimed the land was unoccupied. They reasoned that, because the indigenous people didn't have a civilization or a land use system understandable to Europeans, they didn't count. In 1992, the Australian High Court ruled that *terra nullius* was not valid and that indigenous people had rights to the land that dated back to before Europeans arrived in Australia.

Called the Mabo decision, the opinion is named after Eddie Mabo, a Torres Strait Islander who fought for ten years to have the government acknowledge that his clan owned their traditional land.

The federal government later enacted the Native Title Act, which gives indigenous people the right to their traditional lands. But under this law, people could make claims only on national park lands and some other government lands. The law also required that the indigenous people making the claim continually occupied the land.

Between Two Cultures

The first known Aborigine to become involved with the white settlers was a man named Bennelong of the Iora, or Eora, people. Arthur Phillip, the governor of the New South Wales colony, captured some Aborigines, including Bennelong (right). An intelligent and curious man, Bennelong quickly learned English, and he was able to explain the strange customs of the settlers to his people. Phillip took Bennelong and another Aborigine named Yemmerrawanie to England in 1792. Yemmerrawanie died there, but Bennelong returned to Australia where he served as the go-between for his people and the settlers for several years. Ultimately, however, he found life straddling the two cultures difficult.

British took possession of Western Australia in 1826. Then they established a settlement at Swan River, which became Perth. It became a colony in 1829.

Pushed Aside

The Aborigines did not take kindly to the invasion of their land by white strangers. Within a short time, however, they were dying from diseases brought by the white invaders. They had never before been exposed to these diseases, so their bodies had no natural resistance to them. The Europeans also had guns, and the Aborigines did not. Still, the indigenous people resisted. Windradyne of the Wiradjuri people was remembered for fighting bravely and was undefeated in the field.

Few settlers took the trouble to learn anything about the indigenous people. It was easier to kill them. Colonists under

Governor Sir George Arthur deliberately killed the Aborigines of Tasmania from 1828 to 1832. The few Aborigines who survived were moved to Flinders Island, northeast of Tasmania. Forced from their land, they slowly died.

The settlers gradually took over more and more land on the continent. The indigenous people were moved to the outskirts of towns and cities. Decade by decade, as settlements grew, the number of Aborigines shrank. But indigenous people

Tasmania was a penal colony when George Arthur was governor. He made the prisons more efficient but was also known for his harsh discipline.

continued to live in their traditional manner in sparsely settled areas of the outback and in the Northern Territory and Western Australia. Indeed, Europeans found it impossible to live in much of the nation's inland and tropical north because of the harsh environment. Many Aborigines in these areas did not interact with European Australians—in some cases, not until well into the twentieth century.

Boomerangs were used for hunting by some Aborigines. Others used spears.

In the 1850s, new constitutions in the colonies made Australia more democratic than Britain. These constitutions gave all men the right to vote, regardless of their wealth. Australia also instituted the secret ballot, known to this day as the Australian ballot, so that no one would know how a person had voted.

Greater Freedom

After convicts completed their sentences, they could return home to Britain, though they had to pay their own way. Freed convicts could also choose to establish themselves as free men (or women) in Australia, known as emancipists. About 162,000 prisoners were sent to Australia during the eighty years from 1788 to 1868. These prisoners came from England, Scotland, Wales, Ireland, and other parts of the British Empire, including India, South Africa, and the West Indies. The movement of convicts to Australia was in fact a massive movement of people from around the globe to work and settle the colonies.

By the 1840s, Australian colonists were pressuring the British government to stop transporting convicts to Australia. Some colonists opposed it on moral grounds. They thought it was wrong to send people halfway around the world, often for minor crimes. Others opposed it on economic grounds. Many businesspeople in the colonies thought manufacturing was the key to Australia's future, and having a population of convicts did nothing to advance that. They also wanted greater independence from the British government and new, more democratic constitutions. Britain, having endured the American Revolution and recently given more freedom to Canada, agreed to some of their demands.

Gold!

In 1851, a man named Edward Hargraves started Australia's gold rush. Born in England, Hargraves moved to Australia as a teenager and then traveled to California to search for gold. He soon realized that Australia and California had similar landscapes. He returned home and quickly found gold at Bathurst in New South Wales. Within weeks, Australia's gold rush was on. Fortune hunters from all over the world, including Europe, China, and the United States, descended on the goldfields.

In Britain, some people deliberately got themselves convicted of a crime so they would be transported to the distant land, where they might eventually find riches. In response, the British stopped sending convicts to New South Wales. They continued to send convicts to Western Australia for two more decades, but then gold was found there, too.

The Gold Rush

◇ Goldfields discovered, 1851–1859
◇ 1860–1869
◆ 1870–1889
◆ After 1889

Gold attracted many Chinese to Australia. By 1861, more than thirty-eight thousand people born in China were living in Australia.

The Chinese Arrive

The first known Chinese immigrant to arrive in Australia was a free settler, not a convict. As in the United States, many Chinese immigrants were welcomed as laborers. The promise of gold drew many more.

Chinese immigrants did much of the hard labor in the goldfields. They attracted notice for diligently working old, used sites and other unpromising areas. Some European miners, however, thought the Chinese were too different from themselves. Others were concerned that the Chinese would be willing to work for less money, and this would lower wages for all workers. Deadly riots occurred at Lambing Flat, New South Wales, in 1861, and later in the nineteenth century, there were protests against the arrival of Chinese laborers. Some colonies passed anti-Chinese laws that imposed taxes on the Chinese and restricted their immigration. This was the beginning of what became known as the White Australia policy, which promoted the idea that only Europeans could become Australians.

What Nationality?

By 1860, more than a million Europeans lived in the Australian colonies. Almost from when the colonies were founded, a few farsighted people had thought that the colonies should join as one nation. By the turn of the century, Australians had written a new constitution and come to an agreement that the 3.7 million European Australians would become part of a new nation. Most indigenous Australians, however, were excluded.

In the 1800s, most Australians considered themselves British, not Australian.

Across the Continent

The first Europeans to cross the continent were Robert O'Hara Burke (left), an Irish police officer, and William John Wills (right), a doctor, in 1860. They used camels to travel across the desert. With the help of Aboriginal guides and communities, they made it all the way from Melbourne to the Gulf of Carpentaria in the north. Unfortunately, they were inexperienced and didn't plan well. They died of starvation on the way back to Melbourne.

This was a step backward, because Aboriginal men had been allowed to vote under the colonial constitutions of the 1850s.

The new nation of Australia was officially inaugurated at a gathering in Centennial Park in Sydney in 1901. The people celebrating were at the same time Australian and British. Although they were living in a new nation, they were still British subjects. They had a sense of dual belonging. They loved the country where they lived, but they were also proud of being part of a great world empire. New immigrants kept arriving from Britain and Ireland, and they had a sense of nostalgia for where they had come from. Many people whose families had been in Australia for generations still referred to England as "home."

Yet there was a countertradition that developed in the 1880s and 1890s, fed in part by Irish nationalism brought to Australia by convicts, political prisoners, and immigrants. They did not think that Australians should be proud to be part of an empire that had oppressed people around the world. These ideas were brought to life in the work of the bush poet Henry Lawson, who penned

A statue of Henry Lawson stands in Sydney. He is known for writing about life in the bush.

poems designed to stir Australians to a complete independence. In "A Song of the Republic 1887," he urged Australians to throw off their connections to Britain and its mistakes:

> Sons of the South, awake! arise!
> Sons of the South, and do.
> Banish from under your bonny skies
> Those old-world errors and wrongs and lies.
> Making a hell in a Paradise
> That belongs to your sons and you.

When Britain entered World War I in 1914, patriotism quieted these voices. Australians automatically assumed that they would fight in defense of Britain. Australia lost 59,258 young men out of a total of 330,000 sent abroad. Soldiers from Australia and New Zealand fought together and have since been known as ANZAC (Australian and New Zealand Army Corps) forces.

Australia entered World War II in 1939, when Britain declared war on Germany. Soon Japan entered the war on the side of Germany, and the United States on the side of Britain. Australia was soon exposed to Japanese attack. In 1941, American general Douglas MacArthur and his forces made their base in Melbourne. Australia's prime minister John Curtin made a landmark speech declaring, "Australia looks to America, free of any pangs as to our traditional links or kinship with the United Kingdom."

The Social Laboratory

In the early twentieth century, Australia became known as "the social laboratory of the world" because of its innovative political and social reforms. Women were given the vote. Suffrage groups (left) fought for this right. Pensions were set up to help people when they retired. A special court was established that settled disagreements between employers and workers. A minimum wage was put into place. In part because of these reforms, Australia had much less class conflict than many other nations. The nation proved to be committed to protecting the living standards of its workers and ensuring equality.

With the British focused on fighting Germany and keeping the Japanese out of India, the Japanese appeared to set their sights on Australia. They began advancing on Port Moresby, on the island of New Guinea, which lay on Australia's doorstep. In 1942, Australian troops met the Japanese in the mountains and eventually repelled the Japanese. Today, this is remembered as the Battle for Australia. The Battle of Midway a few months later forced the Japanese to turn their attention away from Australia. Australian soldiers joined Americans in driving the Japanese from the Pacific Islands and Southeast Asia and back to the islands of Japan. By the time the war ended in 1945, about twenty-seven thousand Australian soldiers had died.

Members of the Royal Australian Air Force pose on their bomber in 1941.

Surfers ride the waves near Brisbane in 1964.

Changing Times

After the war ended, Australians gradually moved away from their sense of dual British belonging. This happened for many reasons. One was that the British Empire had broken up. Another was that after the war, people moved to Australia from all over Europe, and they did not look to Britain as the mother country. Australians also became more connected to the United States. American troops had protected them from the Japanese. A new Australian way of life was also emerging. Suburbs were growing. So was a popular culture based on cars, TV, rock 'n' roll, and surfing. These changes drew Australia ever closer to American ways. This closeness was aided by increased U.S. investment in Australia.

In 1975, the governor-general dismissed Gough Whitlam (above), the elected prime minister. This caused further separation of Australia from Britain.

On January 1949, a law went into effect establishing Australian citizenship. The law enabled new European immigrants to become Australian citizens. Aborigines, too, were given citizenship, but they were not counted in the official census. All Australians were still regarded as British subjects.

In 1975, the two houses of parliament were in a deadlock over whether to call new elections. The governor-general, who represents the British queen in her role as the head of state of Australia, broke the deadlock by dismissing the prime minister. This made it clear to Australians that they were still beholden to an unelected official acting in the name of a distant power. It seemed that Australia had not quite escaped its colonial past. A few years later, Australia severed more ties with Britain. The British monarch remains queen of Australia but exercises no real power.

Many Newcomers

After World War II, Australian officials knew they had to increase the country's population or it might fail as a modern nation. They began to invite European immigrants to come in large numbers. Asians were still not welcome to immigrate, though some refugees remained after the war and Asian students began arriving.

Immigrants from many different European countries started coming to Australia. They brought with them things that have since become part of the Australian culture—Italian food, outdoor Mediterranean-style eating, French winemaking techniques, and more. By 1960, more than 1.5 million immigrants had moved to the continent.

As part of Australia's effort to become recognized as a separate, welcoming people, it hosted the Olympics in 1956. It was the first time the Olympic Games had been held outside of Europe or the United States. It was also the first time that they had been televised widely. Swimmer Dawn Fraser, runner Betty Cuthbert, track star John Landy, and other Australians became household names around the world.

Betty Cuthbert (number 468) roars across the finish line to win gold in the 100-meter race at the 1956 Melbourne Olympics.

Postwar prime ministers such as Ben Chifley and Robert Menzies worked to expand the economy. Menzies encouraged Australians to build businesses instead of importing goods from Europe. The United States and other nations started investing in Australia. Menzies also expanded universities to provide skilled professionals to run the country's increasingly complex economy.

Toward the Future

In 1973, Australia ended the last remains of the White Australia policy. A few years later the Vietnam War ended, and Vietnamese refugees began arriving in Australia. These refugees were largely welcomed, and gradually immigration from Asia became a reality. In the 1970s and 1980s, Australia's official policy became multiculturalism, recognizing the right of people of different ethnicities to publicly express their own cultures. The country began to celebrate its diversity as a source of cultural enrichment and economic strength. Today,

Vietnamese refugees arrive in Sydney in 1977.

Australia has strong economic ties to China, and about 3 percent of the population is of Chinese descent.

Thousands of would-be immigrants have arrived on the shores of Australia in recent years. They traveled from Southeast Asia by boat, seeking asylum in Australia. The arrival of these asylum seekers has stirred controversy. Since 2001, the so-called boat people have been placed in detention centers on Christmas Island, small islands off Papua New Guinea, and elsewhere. This is intended to deter future asylum seekers from setting off for Australia. In 2011, a plan was proposed to send new arrivals to Malaysia. Australia, in return, would take in refugees who had been in Malaysia for several years. That plan is not pleasing to anyone, and so at the time of this writing, the fate of the new arrivals remains up in the air. Despite these concerns, Australia remains committed to a multicultural future.

Many people from Sri Lanka have sailed to Australia, seeking asylum.

Governing Australia

THE AUSTRALIAN CONSTITUTION HAS BEEN THE nation's governing framework since the British colonies joined together to become a nation in 1901. The country's name is officially the Commonwealth of Australia. A commonwealth is a community formed for the common good of its members.

Like the United States, Australia is a group of states that joined together in a federation. Each state has its own constitution and is governed in part by state laws. Under the Australian Constitution, some areas, such as foreign relations and defense, are handled exclusively by the national government. Other concerns are handled solely by the states. Many areas, including health and social issues, are handled by both the state and national governments.

Australia is also a constitutional monarchy. The king or queen of the United Kingdom (currently Queen Elizabeth II) is also the king or queen of Australia. The monarch appoints a governor-general to represent him or her in Australia. In theory, the governor-general has a lot of power, but he or she rarely exercises it. The chief role of the governor-general is to be a symbol of the nation outside of politics and to sign legislation into law. Quentin Bryce, the current governor-general,

Opposite: **Queen Elizabeth II is the queen of Australia, but she does not play a significant role in governing the nation.**

Canberra: The Capital City

The name Canberra is probably from an Aboriginal word for "meeting place." In fact, for twenty-one thousand years, the lands around the site of Canberra were home to the Ngunnawal people.

The location of Australia's capital city and the Australian Capital Territory that surrounds it was a compromise. The capital was built in the middle of nowhere, near the border of New South Wales and Victoria, so that it would be about the same distance from Sydney and Melbourne.

The actual land for the capital was donated by New South Wales in 1911. An American from Chicago, Illinois, Walter Burley Griffin, won a competition to design the city. Collaborating with his wife, Marion, he came up with a plan that called for circular patterns of big roads, huge parks spread throughout the city, and a lake in the middle. Construction delays and conflicts between the architect and the government hampered completion of the plan. Canberra did not become a thriving city until the middle of the twentieth century.

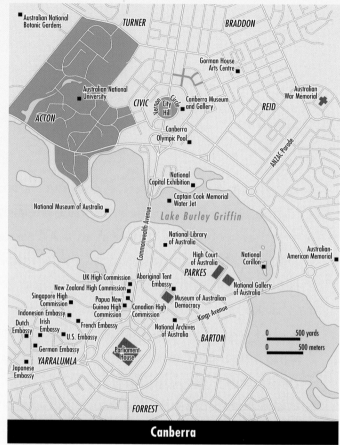

Canberra

Today, Canberra has a population of about 360,000. A permanent parliament building (left) opened in 1988. Since 1972, Aborigines have maintained a "tent embassy" in front of the Old Parliament House (now the Museum of Australian Democracy) to remind the legislature of their grievances.

The Capital Territory includes land beyond Canberra. This territory includes towns such as Yarralumla and Braddon, farms, and even Namadgi National Park. This park has mountains and forests and is part of the larger interconnected Australian Alps National Parks.

is a leading reformer for the status of women and a former governor of Queensland. She is the first woman to hold this office.

The Legislature

Australia's legislature, or lawmaking body, consists of a parliament with two houses. The people elect representatives to parliament. The Senate has seventy-six members, twelve from each state and two from each internal territory. Senators from states are elected to six-year terms, and those from territories are elected to three-year terms. Members of the House of Representatives (MPs or MHRs) are elected for three-year terms from local districts that have equal numbers of voters. The House currently

The Australian House of Representatives meets in Parliament House in Canberra.

The National Anthem

"Advance Australia Fair" officially became Australia's national anthem in 1984, though it had been sung for at least a hundred years before that. It was written by Scottish-born composer Peter Dodds McCormick.

Australians all let us rejoice,
For we are young and free;
We've golden soil and wealth for toil;
Our home is girt by sea;
Our land abounds in nature's gifts
Of beauty rich and rare;
In history's page, let every stage
Advance Australia Fair.
In joyful strains then let us sing,
Advance Australia Fair.

Beneath our radiant Southern Cross
We'll toil with hearts and hands;
To make this Commonwealth of ours
Renowned of all the lands;
For those who've come across the seas
We've boundless plains to share;
With courage let us all combine
To Advance Australia Fair.
In joyful strains then let us sing,
Advance Australia Fair.

has 150 members, but that number can change with population. Members of the House are elected for a term of three years.

In Australia, voting is compulsory. People who do not vote are subject to fines or other penalties. Because of this,

Australia has a very high voter turnout rate. Often, more than 95 percent of eligible voters go to the polls.

Government Leaders

In Australia, the monarch is the head of state. The head of the government is the prime minister. The political party with the most seats in the House of Representatives forms the government and chooses the prime minister. The prime minister is the most powerful figure in the country. He or she appoints the members of the cabinet, who are chosen from both houses of parliament. Each cabinet minister is responsible for a different area of policy, such as trade or health and aging.

Kevin Rudd (back center) addressed members of parliament in 2007, when he was prime minister.

A Female First

Julia Eileen Gillard became Australia's first female prime minister in 2010. Born in Wales, she immigrated to Australia with her family when she was a young child. She grew up to become a lawyer. In 1998, Gillard was elected to the House of Representatives as member of the Labour Party. She served as deputy prime minister before being chosen prime minister. Gillard is not married, but the media call her longtime boyfriend "Australia's first bloke."

The Court System

Court cases in Australia generally start in a state or territory court. Any case can then go on to a federal court.

The nation's highest court is the High Court of Australia. It has a chief justice and six other justices, who are appointed by the prime minister and cabinet. The High Court reviews decisions made in lower courts. Its decisions are final.

The High Court of Australia meets in a modern building that opened in 1980.

AUSTRALIAN NATIONAL GOVERNMENT

Executive Branch

GOVERNOR-GENERAL

PRIME MINISTER

CABINET MEMBERS

Legislative Branch

SENATE

HOUSE OF REPRESENTATIVES

Judicial Branch

HIGH COURT

FEDERAL COURT

FAMILY COURT

FEDERAL MAGISTRATES COURT

Australia has several specialized courts. The Federal Court hears cases involving banks, trade, and industry. Family Court handles cases involving children, families, and divorce. The Federal Magistrates Court is the newest court in the land. It was started in the year 2000. It handles all kinds of cases but in a simpler and quicker way than happens in the federal and family courts.

Expanding Democracy

White women were given the right to vote in federal elections and run for federal office in 1902. The following year, Vida Goldstein, a native of Portland, Victoria, and one of the lead-

Dorothy Tangney served in the Senate for twenty-five years.

ers of Australia's women's rights movement, ran for election to parliament. She was the first woman in the entire British Empire to run for a seat in a federal parliament. Goldstein was defeated, but in 1921 Edith Cowan won a seat in the state parliament of Western Australia.

Enid Lyons of Tasmania became the first woman elected to the federal House of Representatives in 1943. In the same election, Dorothy Tangney of Western Australia was elected to the Senate. Lyons later became the first woman appointed to the cabinet.

The first Aborigine elected to federal parliament was Neville Bonner, a member of the Jagera people from New South Wales.

Australia's Flags

The design of the Australian national flag was chosen by public competition in 1901. The winning flag among 32,823 entries was by five people who submitted similar designs. The flag is a deep blue color. In the upper left is the British flag, called the Union Jack, which features a red and white cross on top of a red and white diagonal cross. Beneath it are several stars. The large star, called the Commonwealth Star, or Federation Star, has seven points for the six states and Northern Territory plus other territories. The other stars make a constellation called the Southern Cross, which is visible only in the Southern Hemisphere.

The official Aboriginal flag shows a yellow sun on horizontal panels of black, which represents the Aboriginal people, and red, which stands for the land. It was designed in 1971 by Harold Thomas of the Luritja people of central Australia.

The Torres Strait Islanders also have an official flag, which was designed by Bernard Namok in 1992. It has a central large panel of blue, symbolizing the water, with top and bottom stripes of green, symbolizing the land. A white five-pointed star represents the five major island groups, and a white headdress represents the people.

He became involved in politics to advance Aboriginal rights. In 1971, the Liberal Party chose him to fill a vacancy in the Senate, and he was later elected several times on his own. In 2010, Ken Wyatt of Hasluck, West Australia, became the first Aborigine elected to the House of Representatives.

Money and Minerals

AUSTRALIA, ONCE A PLACE TO DUMP CONVICTS, later became the biggest wool producer in the world. Since the gold rushes of the 1850s, mining has been important in Australia, and it continues to be central to its economy today.

Australia's economy has been robust in recent years. Most of the rest of the world suffered an economic downturn from 2008 to 2010, but not Australia. During this period, the unemployment rate in the United States rose to 9.1 percent, but in Australia it was just 4.9 percent. Australia was able to weather the downturn because it exports huge amounts of its natural resources to China.

Opposite: **Wheat is the largest crop produced in Australia.**

Growing and Grazing

About half the continent's land is used in agriculture. Most of the agricultural lands are vast grasslands that support huge stations (ranches) where sheep, cattle, and even goats graze. Only about 6 percent of Australia's land is arable, or useful for growing crops. That's the smallest amount of arable land of any country. Australia's main crops are grains such as wheat and barley.

For decades, Australia's major product was wool, which is produced on vast sheep stations. It was said that "Australia rode on the sheep's back." In 2010, there were an estimated seventy-three million sheep in Australia. Today, more than

Sheep graze in New South Wales. More than one-third of all the sheep in Australia are located in New South Wales.

Agriculture (2010)

Wheat	25 million metric tons
Barley	9.3 million metric tons
Sheep	72 million
Beef cattle	25 million

Manufacturing (2008, value in Australian dollars)

Machinery and equipment	$21,073,000,000
Metal products	$20,406,000,000
Food, beverages, and tobacco	$19,787,000,000

Mining (2009)

Iron ore	353 million metric tons
Black coal	333.6 million metric tons
Bauxite	64 million metric tons

70 percent of Australian wool goes to China. Although wool is still important to the economy, other products, especially coal, have topped wool as the main export since 1976.

Australia's newest important agricultural export is wine. Winemaking started in Australia when entrepreneur John Macarthur, who arrived in 1790, planted grapevines from Europe in the Hunter Valley north of Sydney. Immigrants from many parts of the world, including France, Italy, and Germany, brought their knowledge of wine to the continent,

and by 1890, Australia was producing many varieties of wine. Today, Australia is the seventh-largest wine producer in the world and the fourth-largest wine exporter.

Mining and Making

Half of Australia's exports are minerals. Most of the minerals, especially coal and iron ore, are sent to Asian nations.

Australia was long thought to be poor in iron ore—and in most minerals, in fact. But in 1952, Lang Hancock, a native of Perth, discovered a vast supply of high-grade iron ore in the Hamersley Range in the area known as Pilbara. One by one, more minerals were found, turning the area around Perth into the center of a massive mining industry. Rio Tinto, a huge mining business owned by British, Australian, and now Chinese interests, is one of the three largest iron ore producers in the world. Port Hedland in Western Australia is the major shipping point for minerals.

Australia has huge untouched quantities of coal. Victoria most likely has one-fourth of the world's supply of brown coal, which is used to generate power. Brown coal is increasingly unpopular, however, because it creates a great deal of pollution. Queensland has deposits of the kind of coal used to make steel. In addition, it has a fuel called coal seam gas, a natural gas commonly used in Australia. Natural gas is also available in vast quantities under the seabed off Western Australia.

Australia produces huge quantities of liquefied natural gas (LNG), which can be shipped to Asian ports in just a few days. Most of the big power companies of the world are

Mineral Mosts

- The world's largest uranium deposit is at Olympic Dam in South Australia.
- Australia is the largest producer of diamonds in the world. They are mostly industrial diamonds rather than gems, however.
- The world's largest mining company is BHP Billiton, headquartered at Broken Hill in New South Wales. Broken Hill has been mining silver, lead, and zinc since the early twentieth century.
- Australia is by far the world's largest producer of opals.
- Australia produces more bauxite (an iron ore that contains a lot of aluminum) than any other nation. The mine at Cape York is the world's largest.
- Australia exports more coal than any other nation.

Resources

	Symbol	Resource	Symbol	Resource
Cereals (mainly wheat)	Ag	Silver	NG	Natural gas
Dairy and truck farming	Al	Bauxite	Ni	Nickel
Fruit and horticulture	Au	Gold	Pb	Lead
Forests	C	Coal	Sn	Tin
Pasture livestock	Cu	Copper	U	Uranium
Range livestock	D	Diamonds	Zn	Zinc
Nonagricultural land	Fe	Iron ore		Oil

involved in the exploration and development of natural gas in Australia. A project called Gorgon is developing a site in Western Australia that will produce LNG for China, India, Japan, and Korea. It will be the nation's largest export deal.

Australia ranks third in the world in gold production, trailing only China and South Africa. Kalgoorlie in Western Australia has the nation's largest open-pit gold mine.

About one million Australians work in manufacturing. Machinery, metal products, food products, and chemicals are all produced in Australia. Cars are also manufactured in the country. GM-Holden, Ford, and Toyota all have plants there.

The journey across Australia on the Ghan takes about forty-eight hours.

Crossing the Continent

Crossing the dry continent was difficult for early Europeans in Australia. Beginning in 1860, they brought in camels to help them explore and develop the desert regions. The camels were trained and handled by Afghans, people from central

Australia's Airman

Charles Kingsford Smith, who was born in Brisbane, began his flying career as a fighter pilot during World War I. In 1921, he became one of the first pilots to fly for Western Australian Airways, the country's first airline. He flew mail in the outback for several years, and then in 1928 broke distance records by flying from San Francisco, California, to Brisbane, via Honolulu, Hawaii, and Fiji. Later, his plane went down in Kimberley, Western Australia. Another plane that was sent to look for him had to make an emergency landing, and its crew died. Kingsford Smith and his crew were eventually found. After years of breaking more records, he disappeared in 1935 during an attempt to break the speed record between Australia and England.

Asia who followed the religion of Islam. The Afghans used camels to help lay telegraph lines, explore for gold, and build railways. Even today, the world's longest north-south railway, which runs 1,800 miles (2,900 km) from Adelaide to Darwin, is called the Ghan in memory of the Afghan cameleers.

The Indian Pacific railroad, which opened in 1970, is the second-longest rail line in the world. It takes three days to cross Australia from Sydney to Perth, a distance of 2,704 miles (4,352 km).

In 1925, a car made it around Australia for the first time, traveling from Perth to Melbourne and back again. Today, most people get around the country in cars. Many people drive pickup trucks, which are called utes, short for utility vehicles.

Australia's national airline is Qantas Airways. The name is a shortened version of its original name, Queensland and Northern Territory Aerial Services. Formed in 1920 in Winton, Queensland, it is the oldest continuously operating airline in the world.

Qantas carries about two-thirds of all passengers flying within Australia.

Nobel Prize Winners

Several Australians have won the Nobel Prize, the world's most prestigious award, for their scientific research. The youngest Nobel Prize winner ever was William Lawrence Bragg, who won the prize in physics in 1915 at the age of twenty-five. This North Adelaide native was only twenty-two when he discovered a way to determine the crystal structure of a material. Howard Florey, a native of Adelaide, was awarded the Nobel Prize in Physiology (medicine) in 1945 for his work developing penicillin, a medicine that treats infections. Barry Marshall and J. Robin Warren were awarded the prize in physiology in 2005 for their work showing the role of bacteria in ulcers. The only Australian woman to

win the Nobel Prize is Elizabeth H. Blackburn (above) of Tasmania, who won in 2009 for her research into chromosomes.

Australia's main aircraft manufacturer, the Commonwealth Aircraft Corporation, started making military aircraft in 1936. It is now part of Boeing, an American company.

Science and Engineering

The Commonwealth Scientific and Industrial Research Organisation (CSIRO) concerns itself with all aspects of science and its impact on the Australian economy, environment, and society. CSIRO scientists explore the heavens with several world-class radio telescopes and persuade Australians to eat healthily, providing recipes for them to use. It even spreads traditional Aboriginal knowledge. For example, the scientists of CSIRO have investigated the way Aborigines managed wetlands in the north, as well as how they prevented insect

Worldwide Newsman

Rupert Murdoch, media mogul, is a native of Melbourne. He inherited one newspaper, the *Adelaide Advertiser*, from his father, Sir Keith Murdoch, a renowned journalist and publisher. In 1964, Rupert started a national daily newspaper called the *Australian*. He turned international by buying two British papers, the *Sun* and the *News of the World*.

In 1979, Murdoch founded News Corporation, one of the largest communications companies in the world. It owns such famous businesses as the Fox Broadcasting Company and many newspapers, most importantly the *Wall Street Journal*. His Satellite Television Asia Region (STAR) covers much of Asia, including greater China.

In 2011, Murdoch shut down the 168-year-old *News of the World* after it was discovered that reporters were hacking into people's cell phones.

infestations. CSIRO is also working with Torres Strait fishermen to manage marine fisheries. Sea cucumbers, for example, were long traded by indigenous people and are now harvested for export to Asia, where they are considered a delicacy.

Australia has more than five hundred dams that collect water for irrigation and harness it for hydroelectric power. Australia has no nuclear power plants, but it has one-third the world's supply of uranium, a mineral used to produce nuclear power. Many Australians do not want their nation to explore nuclear power, a type of power that can be dangerous, because they have a plentiful supply of coal.

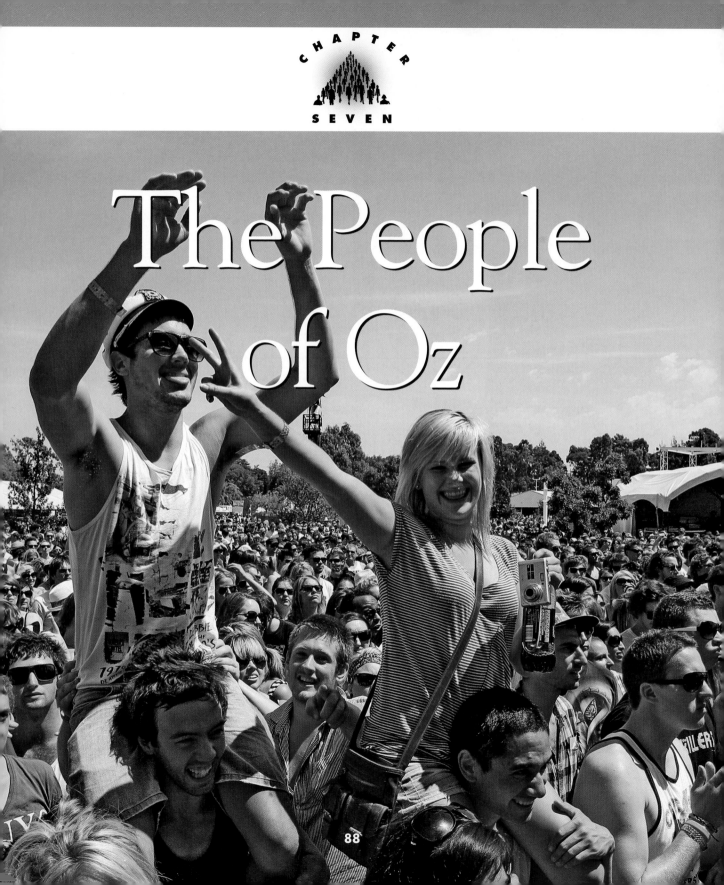

CHAPTER

SEVEN

The People of Oz

AUSTRALIA IS OFTEN CALLED OZ. SO THE PEOPLE of Australia are called Ozzies, not Aussies.

Australia is the sixth-largest nation in area in the world. In population, however, it is only fifty-first. In October 2011, it had an estimated 22,743,461 people.

Although Australia is a big country, most of its people live along the eastern and southern coasts, in cities within about 30 miles (50 km) of the sea. Nine-tenths of Australians live in cities, making it the fourth most urban nation on earth. Few urban people ever venture into the outback, although many enjoy spending time in the closer inland bush and on the long coastal stretches of beaches and lakes.

The Original Australians

Europeans called the native people of Australia Aborigines, from the word *aboriginal*, meaning "being the first of a kind in a region." The Aborigines are not all one group, however. They belong to many different groups, such as the Nunga in South

Opposite: **Australians enjoy a concert in Melbourne.**

Persons per square mile		Persons per square kilometer
more than 64		more than 24
25–64		10–24
3–24		1–9
fewer than 3		fewer than 1
uninhabited		uninhabited

Australia and the Nyungar in the southern part of Western Australia. Linguists, people who study language, think that Australia's Aboriginal people spoke up to 250 languages before the European settlers came. Today, only about 15 of those languages are still used.

Aborigines are not the only indigenous Australians. The Torres Strait Islanders come from the islands that lie between Australia and New Guinea. They are a distinct group of people who speak a variety of languages. Some of these languages are related to Aboriginal languages of the mainland and some to island languages. Torres Strait Islanders emphasize their distinct culture and customs, which are based on the environments of the islands and the sea. But many, like the indigenous rights campaigner Eddie Mabo, came to live on the mainland, mostly in northern Queensland.

Population of Major Cities (2011 est.)

Sydney	4,596,328
Melbourne	4,092,430
Brisbane	2,056,290
Adelaide	1,206,899
Perth	1,554,769

The Stolen Generations

Beginning in 1909, it was the policy of the Australian government to take Aboriginal children of mixed descent from their Aboriginal mothers. These children were abducted by government authorities and placed in schools, missions, or sometimes with white families, where they could learn to

The Boomerang

The boomerang is a club associated with the Aborigines, but it did not originate in Australia. It probably arrived in Australia from Indonesia with the first native people. It may have originally come from India. The most famous boomerang is the returning boomerang. It is curved in such a way that, when thrown, it flies in a big arc and returns to the person who threw it. The thrower uses the boomerang to strike a kangaroo, a flying bird, or even an enemy.

become part of white society. Many people believe that the government officials did this because they wanted Aboriginal traditions and languages to die out. The members of the "stolen generations" were not told their parents' names, and most never saw their mothers again.

Members of the Stolen Generations, who as children were taken away from their families, listen to Prime Minister Kevin Rudd's speech of apology for the tragic treatment by the government.

Prime Minister Rudd apologized on behalf of the Australian government to the tens of thousands of members of the Stolen Generations.

This experiment was not abandoned until 1970. While long lamented by indigenous Australians who lost loved ones, the government did not acknowledge it as a great wrong until 1997, with the *Bringing Them Home Report*. This report caused great sadness and anger among Australians of all backgrounds, and many leaders publicly apologized on behalf of state governments. Still, Australian prime minister John Howard declined to officially apologize. This upset many indigenous people and other Australians. Then, in 2008, Prime Minister Kevin Rudd made a clear apology to the indigenous people before the Australian Parliament. He said, "For the pain, suffering and hurt of these Stolen Generations, their descendants and for their families left behind, we say sorry. To the mothers and the fathers, the brothers and the sisters, for the breaking up of families and communities, we say sorry."

People of all backgrounds have worked toward reconciliation, or forgiveness. While acknowledging the mistreatment of the indigenous people, they are working toward a better future. As part of this effort, about a million Australians took part in the People's Walk for Reconciliation across the Sydney Harbour Bridge.

In 2000, many Australians participated in the Walk for Reconciliation across Sydney Harbour Bridge.

Aborigines were not the only children taken from their parents. In the two decades after World War II, British officials took perhaps ten thousand British children, often as young as three years old, from poor or troubled homes in Britain and shipped them to Australia. The children had no idea where they were going or why. They were told they were going to happy homes. Instead, they arrived to find themselves not with families, but in large camps where they had to work and received no education. Not until they were adults did they learn that many of them had families hoping to get them back. In 2009, the Australian government apologized to these children.

Thousands of British children were shipped to Australia in the years after World War II.

A census worker helps another Australian fill out a census form.

Counting Australians

The Australian constitution calls for a census, or count, of the people every five years. The last one took place in 2011. Today, 92 percent of Australians are of European descent, 7 percent are Asian, and 1 percent is "other." Most people of Asian descent have Chinese, Indian, Vietnamese, or Filipino heritage. Today, many Asian Australians marry European Australians. The fastest-growing ethnic category of Australians is "mixed."

Life expectancy for a non-Aboriginal Australian is 81.8 years, the ninth-longest of any country in the world. Women live about five years longer than men. Aboriginal people, however, live an average of seventeen years less than other Australians. This difference is primarily because of poverty and inadequate health care.

Ethnic Australia

European	92%
Asian	7%
Aborigine or Torres Strait Islander	2%
Other	1%

Immigration

Like the United States and Canada, Australia is a nation of immigrants. In the twentieth century, the government decided that the country should have a larger population. It started to invite people from other countries to immigrate. Many people moved from Europe, Asia, and the Middle East. In the decades after World War II, the national policy of trying to keep Australia white gradually ended. It has been replaced by a welcoming multiculturalism.

An estimated three hundred thousand immigrants arrived in Australia in 2008, though many were probably temporary workers. In the past, most temporary workers eventually became permanent residents. Today, it's not easy to immigrate to Australia. Immigrants have to be part of a family that is already there or have an occupation or business skills that Australia requires. If immigrants come to Australia independently, they have to pass a test demonstrating that they can read and speak English.

Mad Max Mush

The Australian accent can sometimes be hard for people from other countries, such as the United States, to understand. The actors' accents in the popular Australian film *Mad Max* were so thick that movie studio officials thought Americans wouldn't be able to understand them. So when the movie was released in the United States in 1979, the dialogue was replaced by actors speaking with American accents. In 2002, a DVD containing the original dialogue was released in the United States.

An Aborigine guide leads a
tour near Uluru/Ayers Rock.

Language

In 2006, 16 percent of the people in Australia spoke a language other than English at home. The six most common were Italian, Greek, Arabic, Cantonese, Mandarin, and Vietnamese. Both Cantonese and Mandarin are Chinese languages.

Some Aborigines still speak their traditional languages. The Australian map is filled with place names that came from

Speaking Australian

barbie	barbecue	g'day	hello, good day
beaut	wonderful!	go walkabout	disappear unexpectedly
brumby	wild horse	jackaroo	station hand
cobber	friend	jumbuck	sheep
crook	ill, or badly made	never never	the outback
fair dinkum	genuine	sparky	electrician
fair go	an equal chance	strewth!	gee whiz
footy	football		

indigenous words, such as Nambucca, Yarra Yarra, Ettalong, and Bungle Bungle. In 1993, a law passed requiring that places have two official names, one Aboriginal and one English. The first place to become double named was Uluru/Ayers Rock.

Some Aboriginal words have become part of everyday Australian English. Aboriginal languages are the origin of many plant and animal names, including kangaroo, wombat, mulga, and koala. Another Aboriginal term that has become widespread is willy willy, a swirling tower of dust-filled wind in the desert.

In parts of the Northern Territory, a language called Kriol is used. It is a vibrant combination of English, several Aboriginal languages, and Chinese. Today, it is regarded as a language of its own because its structure and grammar are different from standard English.

The spelling of words in Australian English is a mix of American English and British English, although the grammar rules are generally British. Many words that in the United States end with an "or" will end with an "our" in Australia.

Waltzing Matilda

The song "Waltzing Matilda" is so associated with Australia that some people think it is the national anthem. But it is in fact a folk song that was written in 1895 by a poet named Banjo Paterson (left). The music, written by Christina Macpherson, was based on a Scottish melody. The lyrics tell the story of a tramp ("swagman") who steals and eats a sheep ("jumbuck"). When the police go after him, he drowns himself in a small lake ("billabong"). The phrase "waltzing matilda" refers to someone who is traveling with his possessions in a swag, a thin rolled sleeping mattress with a few possessions inside.

Examples include *colour* and *humour*. In Australia, hair turns *grey*, not *gray*. Australians play *chequers*, not *checkers*. And they *organise* their schedules instead of *organizing* them.

In Australia, a whirling cloud of dust is called a willy willy.

Spiritual Life

AUSTRALIA HAS NO OFFICIAL RELIGION. WHEN THE nation was formed at the beginning of the twentieth century, the constitution prevented the government from interfering with anyone's practice of religion or from establishing a religion for the nation.

Australia is not a very religious society. Many Christians do not attend church very often. And almost one-third of Australians do not identify themselves as belonging to any particular religion. This number is steadily increasing.

Aborigine Traditions

Traditionally, the spiritual life of Australia's indigenous people was closely tied to their daily life. The spirits decreed how they should live, when they should move with the changing seasons, how to heal injuries or illnesses, and what stories they should tell their children and when they should tell them.

This is all related to the Dreaming, or Dreamtime. This was, for Aborigines, how creation began and when their ways of life were determined. All individuals exist in the Dreaming both before and after their time on earth. Individual tribes and clans tell their own versions of the Dreaming.

The land is at the heart of Aboriginal belief and life. The land is always present and is basically unchanging, while people change all the time. Their land is their identity. Some Aborigines say the land is their mother or that the land owns them. This is one reason it was so devastating to Aborigines when European settlers claimed land that the Dreaming spirits said was theirs. Many sites remain sacred to Aborigines.

A young man fishes in Northern Territory. This region is filled with sites sacred to the Ganalbingu people.

The Origins of Ancient Stories

Scientists have discovered that some Aboriginal tales must have originated at least ten thousand years ago. They can date specific events, such as volcanic eruptions, that are described in the tales still told today. Some of these tales also tell of a coastal forest overlooking the Great Barrier Reef. That forest is no longer visible because at the end of the last ice age, about ten thousand years ago, the oceans rose, and water covered it.

Although most Aborigine nations have different myths and spirit beings, the spirit known as Rainbow Serpent is found in most Aborigine religions. Rainbow Serpent is considered responsible for the creation of human beings. He also shaped the land itself when he came out of hiding underground and moved across the continent, forming mountains here or rivers there.

In traditional Aborigine religions, spirits or people practicing evil spells are said to cause illness. Even slight accidents are said to be caused by evil thinking on the part of someone else. Healers, or spiritual doctors, "sing" cures to illnesses. Such healing is still used in the outback today, sometimes in combination with modern medicine.

Aborigines perform traditional rituals at a gathering called a *corroboree*. People wear paint and costumes during a corroboree. They dance and sing, interacting with the spirit beings in the Dreaming. Often several clans that don't normally interact will gather at a corroboree, especially when food is plentiful. Outsiders are usually not permitted to watch these events.

The Anglican Church is the largest Protestant church in Australia.

Religions in Australia (2006)

Roman Catholic	25.8%
Anglican	18.7%
Other Christian	19.4%
No Religion	18.7%
Buddhist	2.1%
Muslim	1.75%
Hindu	0.7%
Jewish	0.4%
Other non-Christian 0.5%	

*Note: 11.9% did not answer the question on which religion they follow.

Today, few Aborigines practice their traditional religion. Most are now Christian.

Christianity Comes to Australia

When convicts and their overseers came to Australia, they brought their religion with them. Thus, the Anglican Church, or Church of England, was the primary religion of the early settlers. Anglicanism became less popular in the twentieth century. Today, there are about 3.7 million Anglicans in Australia. Other early settlers brought different Protestant beliefs, including Presbyterianism and Methodism.

The Irish brought Catholicism to Australia. Catholicism became even more common in the twentieth century, when many people immigrated to Australia from Italy and other predominantly Catholic countries. St. Mary's Cathedral in

Sydney is regarded as the head church in Australia. The only Australian to be declared a saint is Mary MacKillop, canonized in 2010. Born in Fitzroy, Victoria, in 1842, she founded an educational order of Catholic nuns in South Australia.

Other Religions

Islam came to Australia as a permanent religion when Afghan camel drivers arrived in the nineteenth century. The first lasting mosque, a Muslim house of worship, was built in 1888 at Adelaide. Today, Islam is growing rapidly, primarily because of the many immigrants from the Middle East, Indonesia, and Malaysia. Some Aborigines have converted to Islam because it has some similarities to their traditional religion. Other Aborigines find it appealing because, unlike Christianity, it is not associated with the European settlers who oppressed them.

The gold rush brought Buddhists from China to Australia in large numbers. A temple used by Buddhists and others was built in Melbourne in 1856. Today, many European Australians are also interested in Buddhism.

Buddhist monks perform a ceremony in Brisbane. Buddhism is a growing religion in Australia.

Arts and Sports

THE CULTURE AND TALENTS OF THE PEOPLE OF Australia have reached around the world. Australian movie actors are known almost everywhere. So are Australian singers. The didgeridoo, an instrument some Aborigines use in traditional ceremonies, makes a foghorn-like sound. It is now played by children across the globe.

Australian Voices

The Warumpi Band, formed in the Northern Territory in 1980, recorded the first rock music in an Aboriginal language. An Aboriginal singer named Geoffrey Gurrumul Yunupingu, who was born blind, plays the guitar, drums, and didgeridoo, and sings soulful songs in his native language, Yolngu. His records and YouTube appearances are popular worldwide.

Two of the greatest early female opera stars came from Australia. Nellie Melba (for whom Melba toast and the dessert peach Melba were named) was born in Richmond, Victoria. She sang on stages the world over in the late nineteenth and early twentieth centuries, often performing with the great

Italian singer Enrico Caruso. In 1927, *Time* magazine called her the "only world-famed Australian." In later decades, Joan Sutherland, a native of Sydney, became a renowned opera star. She won Grammy Awards for her album *The Art of the Prima Donna*.

Popular music owes much to Australia, too. Olivia Newton-John and the Bee Gees were among the most popular performers of the 1970s. AC/DC, an Australian rock band formed in 1973, has the second–best-selling album of all time, *Back in Black*. Kylie Minogue, a child actress-turned-singer, is a native of Melbourne. She was once voted Australia's most

AC/DC is one of the most popular rock bands of all time. The group has sold more than two hundred million records.

popular television performer. Keith Urban was born in New Zealand but raised in Australia. He's been singing in the United States since 2000. Cody Simpson is a singer-songwriter from Gold Coast, Queensland. In 2009, at age fourteen, he started promoting his songs via YouTube. He soon signed a recording contract with Atlantic Records.

Hugh Jackman is a popular actor, singer, and dancer. He has appeared in such films as *X-Men* and *Australia*.

Movie Australia

Many successful movie actors grew up in Australia. They include Russell Crowe, Cate Blanchett, Nicole Kidman, Naomi Watts, Geoffrey Rush, Heath Ledger, and Hugh Jackman. Errol Flynn, the romantic swashbuckling hero of 1930s and 1940s movies, was born in Hobart, Tasmania.

Director Gillian Armstrong has made American movies such as *Little Women* and Australian movies such as *My Brilliant Career.*

Australia has also produced many successful film directors. Peter Weir was nominated for an Academy Award for *Witness*, and Bruce Beresford's film *Driving Miss Daisy* won one. Several female directors have also made their mark, including Gillian Armstrong, who directed such films as *Little Women* and *Mrs. Soffel.*

Writers

For decades, Australians wanted to read only materials brought from Europe, but when they began to develop their own country, they also developed their own literature. In the nineteenth century, Marcus Clarke wrote *For the Term of His Natural Life*, which tells the story of a convict sent to Australia. Henry Lawson wrote bush ballads and short stories. A woman named Miles Franklin wrote *My Brilliant Career*, a novel about an independent girl growing up in rural Australia.

A good way to get to know the Australian landscape and themes is in the books of Nevil Shute, who moved from Britain to Australia in 1950. In his most famous novel, *On the*

Beach, Australia is the last surviving outpost from radioactive fallout after a global nuclear war. A U.S. submarine crew takes refuge in Melbourne as the deadly fallout slowly moves south, toward them.

In 1964, Kathleen Jean Mary Ruska (Kath Walker) became the first indigenous Australian to publish a book of poetry, *We Are Going*. After she became famous, she wanted to honor her heritage, so she began using her indigenous name, Oodgeroo Noonuccal.

Nevil Shute was born in England and moved to Australia as an adult. Many of his books are set in Australia.

Patrick White, who was born in Britain but was a lifelong resident of Sydney, pioneered Australian modernist writing. In 1973, he became the only Australian to win the prestigious Nobel Prize in Literature.

Thomas Keneally, a native of Sydney, wrote the novel that became the Oscar-winning film *Schindler's List*, about a businessman who defies the Nazis and helps rescue Jews during World War II. Keneally often writes about Australia. In *The Chant of Jimmie Blacksmith*, he deals with relations between Aborigines and European Australians.

Australia's best-known novelist, Peter Carey, frequently delves into the country's history. In his award-winning books such as *Oscar and Lucinda* and *True History of the Kelly Gang*, he brings to life Australia's unusual past.

Notorious Ned Kelly

Some people think Ned Kelly was a violent outlaw. Others think of him as a Robin Hood–type hero. Either way, Kelly is a popular Australian folk hero. He was a type of colonial highwayman known as a bush-ranger. His father was a convict, thief, and murderer. In Victoria in the 1870s, he became the leader of the notorious Kelly Gang. Kelly claimed to be fighting injustice imposed on poor Irish Australians, and many ordinary people near Victoria supported him. This area is still known as Kelly Country.

The police finally caught up with the Kelly Gang in Glenrowan. Kelly and his men emerged from a pub wearing "armor" made of metal plow parts. But the armor didn't cover Kelly's legs, and the police shot him. He was tried, found guilty, and executed in 1880. His last words were "Such is life."

Artists

Perhaps the most celebrated Aboriginal artist is Albert Namatjira, who was born near Alice Springs in 1902. He is best known for his watercolors that depict the outback.

Many people prefer the more symbolic art of today's Aboriginal artists. Clifford Possum Tjapaltjarri and other artists made dot paintings, which tell stories in colorful designs, more like the rock paintings and sand maps that Aborigines made long ago. In dot painting, shapes are defined by lines of dots of different colors. Such painting grew out of people making pictures on sand, using seeds, flowers, and other materials.

When many European artists came to Australia, they found that their old skills did not capture the light and landscape of Australia. They had to experiment with new paints

Albert Namatjira made detailed paintings of the Australian landscape.

and colors. In the 1880s and 1890s, impressionist painters in a group called the Heidelberg School began trying to depict the light and color of the bush and the seaside. By the early twentieth century, the Heidelberg School was firmly established as a national movement depicting life in Australia.

Sidney Nolan, a native of Carlton, began painting with a group of revolutionary expressionists and surrealists in the 1930s and 1940s. Their work expressed heightened emotion. By the 1950s, Nolan had established an international reputation. He often painted Australian historical figures and is particularly remembered for a series depicting Ned Kelly, the legendary bushranger.

One of Sidney Nolan's greatest achievements is a large mural on copper depicting a miners' rebellion known as the Eureka Stockade. It now adorns the Reserve Bank of Australia building in Melbourne.

Reg Mombassa

You can see the art of Reg Mombassa everywhere. It's on T-shirts, and it's in museums. His work adorns the Mambo surfwear label, so you can see it on beach clothes. He also paints buildings and people. He typically uses large blocks of color, so his paintings have a cartoonlike quality. Mombassa was a guitarist in a popular band called Mental As Anything, one of the most popular bands in Australia in the 1980s.

Sports

Author Robert Hughes called sports "the real religion" of Australia. Name a sport and Australians play it.

Cricket came to Australia with the British. It's a game a bit like baseball, but some types of cricket matches go on for days. Australia's national team is one of the oldest in the world. They've won the Cricket World Cup four times, more than any other country. One player, Donald Bradman, called "the Don," scored so often that he is considered the greatest batsman ever.

In New South Wales and Queensland, rugby, a type of football, is popular. Australia plays soccer (called national association football) internationally and locally. The national team has reached the finals of the World Cup three times but has never won.

Many Australians, especially Victorians, prefer Australian rules football, or footy. It looks a bit like a rough combination of soccer and American football, although some people think

A Hero of a Horse

Phar Lap is Australia's most famous Thoroughbred racehorse. Born in New Zealand, he was trained and raced in Australia in the early years of the Great Depression in the 1930s, and his story and his success distracted people from their economic troubles. He was an ugly duckling. But despite his funny looks, his breeding indicated that he should be a good racer. And he was. He won thirty-seven of his fifty-one races.

it has Aboriginal origins. Each team has twenty-two members, and eighteen are on the field at any one time. Players can use any part of their body to move the ball toward the goal posts, but they cannot throw the ball. If they run with the ball, they must bounce it or touch it on the ground every 48 feet (15 m), giving the game a basketball feel.

The Australian Open is one of tennis's four Grand Slam tournaments, the sport's most prestigious contests. One of the greatest tennis players ever was Rod Laver, from Queensland. He was number one in the world for seven years in a row, from 1964 to 1970. Evonne Goolagong, a native of New South Wales, was the first world-famous Aborigine. She won fourteen Grand Slam titles during her career, including four Australian Opens in the 1970s and early 1980s.

Australians love horse racing. They will watch impromptu races in rough tracks in the outback, or spend lots of money betting on the nation's top race, the Melbourne Cup. It has been held every November since 1861. Only one horse, Makybe Diva, has won three times, in 2003, 2004, and 2005.

Australia has participated in every Summer Olympics since the competition began. It has also hosted the Summer Olympics twice, in Melbourne in 1956 and in Sydney in 2000. The Sydney Games were well-organized and a huge success. The head of the International Olympic Committee called them the best Games ever.

Aboriginal sprinter Cathy Freeman lit the Olympic flame in the opening ceremony of the Sydney Games. She ran a lap around the stadium carrying both the Aboriginal flag and the Australian flag.

Overall, Australian Olympians have done best in swimming. Dawn Fraser, who was born in New South Wales in 1937, took part in three Olympic Games starting in 1956, winning a total of four gold medals and four silver medals. She is one of only two swimmers to win the same event three Olympics in a row.

The Australian Crawl

The front crawl or freestyle, one of the four basic swimming strokes, is often called the Australian crawl. Europeans, who traditionally did the breaststroke, first saw it being done by Native Americans in the mid-1800s, and they thought it was very "un-European." Australian swimmers perfected the stroke and made it famous. Today, swimmers everywhere use it because it is the fastest stroke.

The Way of Life

AUSTRALIAN AUTHOR ROBERT HUGHES WROTE: "The 'typical Australian' is not, as foreigners once thought, a bushman. He is a slightly worried guy with a tan, a bald spot, a mortgage, a mower and two kids, whose Australian dream is a double-front brick bungalow on a quarter-acre lot in the suburbs less than 30 minutes' drive from the nearest beach."

That sounds a lot like a "typical American," and in many ways it is. But in some ways, Australians are different from Americans. Australians are extremely relaxed and down to earth. They are so informal, in fact, that many call the prime minister by his or her first name.

Opposite: **For many Australians, going to the beach is an everyday part of life.**

Going to School

The school year begins in late January, which is summer in Australia. Most schools have four terms, with a couple of weeks off between terms. They get a long break in the middle of winter and an even longer one during the summer, when they can spend Christmas on the beach!

All children must start school by age six, but many begin going to kindergarten at age three or four. Middle school is grades 7, 8, and 9, and senior school, or high school, is grades 10, 11, and 12. In Tasmania, children must attend school until they are sixteen; in all of the other states, children must remain in school until age fifteen. Most children, however, stay in school through grade 12.

At least 80 percent of Australia's high school graduates go on to college. College can be a university, a technical school, or a vocational school.

The number of students going to school beyond grade 12 has increased greatly in recent decades. In 1940, there were only about fourteen thousand university students in Australia. Today, more than a million students attend thirty-nine uni-

School of the Air

Adelaide Miethke worked for a medical service in the outback. She noticed that all outback children learned to use the radio in case of emergency. She suggested that they could also use radios for education. The idea was tried in Alice Springs in 1948, and it was a success. The School of the Air officially began in 1951, broadcasting from Adelaide. In 2003, the school switched to using wireless Internet for classes.

The school in Alice Springs has been called the world's largest classroom. It has 120 students spread over more than 500,000 square miles (1.3 million sq km). About one-fourth of the students are Aborigines. A student usually spends about an hour a day work-

ing with a teacher over the Internet and then several more hours doing work, supervised by a parent or older sibling.

versities. About 20 percent of all university students are international students, mostly from China and India.

Open Universities Australia allows anyone in Australia to take courses for higher education or professional development. In 2009, more than forty-nine thousand students were enrolled. The courses are provided by regular universities, but they are transmitted over the Internet.

For many young Australians, education is not complete without a "grand tour" of the northern part of the world. They try to visit Asia, Europe, and North America before settling down in that "double-front brick bungalow." Indeed, Australians are great travelers. Many travel the world with a backpack when they are young. When they get older, many go on family holidays to some distant land or take jobs as skilled workers overseas.

About forty thousand students attend the University of Queensland. Its main campus is in St. Lucia, a suburb of Brisbane.

Flying Doctors

John Flynn (1880–1951), a Presbyterian minister from Moliagul, Victoria, worked in very remote areas. He realized that airplanes could bring medical care to these places, so he founded the Royal Flying Doctor Service (RFDS). People living far from a town could call by shortwave radio to get a doctor to fly in to take care of serious medical emergencies. Their radios were powered by pumping pedals (a method invented by Australian Alfred Traeger), so that batteries were not needed. Today, the RFDS flies sixty aircraft out of twenty-one bases throughout the country and takes care of more than 270,000 patients each year.

The Beckoning Beach

Bathing in the warm sea became popular almost as soon as European settlers—who were used to cold oceans—began coming to Australia. Today, almost all Australians swim at one of the thousands of beaches that line the shores of the continent. Probably the most famous is Bondi Beach near Sydney.

In several places along the coast, fast and dangerous currents occur in the waters where people swim. Called rip currents, they form when waves hitting the shore are forced sideways until they find an exit back into the ocean. Swimmers can be caught in rip currents and pulled out into the ocean. Lifeguards called surf lifesavers are taught how to rescue people from rips, and they regularly train and compete in water endurance rescue activities known as ironman tournaments.

Surfing is hugely popular in Australia. The nation has some of the best surfing spots in the world, including Bells Beach in Victoria. Boogie boarding is also popular. A boogie board is like a short surfboard. Instead of standing on the board, riders lie on it and ride the waves into shore.

Surfing is wildly popular in Australia.

Watching the Screen

More than three-quarters of all Australian homes have access to the Internet. Fewer Aborigine and Torres Strait Islander children have computers at home, but most can access them at school.

Down Down Down

Down Down Down is a game of catch played in Australia. Two players toss a ball, such as a tennis ball, back and forth. They stand far enough apart that catching is not always easy. When a player fails to catch the ball, she goes down on one knee and must remain that way. If she drops the ball again, she drops down to the other knee. What comes next? She goes down on one elbow, and then the second elbow, which makes catching the ball very difficult. A player loses when she is lying flat on the ground.

The federal government began a program in 2008 to put a laptop in the hands of every Australian student in high school.

Younger children tend to play games on the Internet, while older ones use it for socializing. In 2011, about half of all Australians were using Facebook to communicate with each other.

Australia is putting in place a new national network bringing fiber optic cable to every home and business in Australia. This will likely create the fastest Internet service in the world.

People fill sidewalk cafés on a warm day in Sydney.

Let's Eat Lamingtons

What's a Lamington? It's a small square of sponge cake with chocolate icing and coconut dusted over it. No one's quite sure where it came from. Perhaps it was a favorite of Lord Lamington, the governor of Queensland at the end of the nineteenth century. Or perhaps not. To Australians, the origin doesn't matter. They just know that Lamingtons are good to eat and easy to make.

To make Lamingtons, you can begin by making a nice buttery cake. But it's easier to buy a sponge cake or pound cake and cut it into small squares, about 1 inch across.

Frosting ingredients

1 pound confectioners' sugar

$\frac{1}{3}$ cup cocoa

3 tablespoons softened, unsalted butter

$\frac{1}{2}$ cup milk

3 cups shredded dried unsweetened coconut

Directions

Sift the sugar and cocoa together into a bowl. Add the butter and milk. Put the bowl into a pan of hot water, and stir the mixture until the frosting is smooth and shiny.

Holding each square of cake on a fork, dip it into the frosting. Hold it over the bowl while the excess frosting drips off. Sprinkle each square liberally with coconut. Place the cake pieces on a rack to harden. Enjoy!

Good to Eat

Traditionally, Australian food was British food. When immigrants began arriving from other parts of the world, they brought their own cuisine with them. Today, Australian meals might show the influence of Thai, Chinese, Japanese, Indian, French, and especially Mediterranean cooking. The basic foods have not changed. For example, many kinds of fish are available along the coasts, but they are now prepared in many different ways.

Some Aboriginal people living in remote areas eat traditional indigenous foods, such as kangaroo, emu, turtle, and shellfish, but a Western diet is increasingly common. Urban Aborigines are unlikely to eat any indigenous food at all.

Since 1993, it has been legal to sell kangaroo meat in Australia. It is now available in supermarkets and small meat markets. Some is exported, particularly to Europe. Kangaroo meat is higher in protein and lower in fat than beef. Kangaroo has long been used in dog food in Australia, which makes some people hesitant to eat it.

A chef prepares kangaroo meat. Kangaroo is typically considered a tender meat and has a strong flavor.

Australians are among the biggest eaters of chocolate in the world. When Oxfam, a British charitable organization, surveyed 16,000 people in developed countries about their favorite foods, only Australians put chocolate at the top of their list. The little chocolate-covered cakes called Lamingtons are especially popular.

Vegemite is the subject of jokes around the world, but most Australians love it. It is a brown, rather salty food paste made from brewer's yeast. Vegemite spread thinly on bread is the favorite sandwich of most Australian children. Vegemite was invented in Melbourne in 1922 with the hope that it would replace the similar British spread called Marmite. Today, almost twenty-three million jars of Vegemite, now owned by the American company Kraft, are sold each year.

Australians are always ready to invite friends over to a barbecue, or barbie. They might serve sausages, lamb chops, steak, prawns (shrimp), or something more exotic. Gathering around the barbie brings out the natural friendliness of the people of Australia.

Australian National Holidays	
New Year's Day	January 1
Australia Day	January 26
Good Friday and Easter Monday	March or April
ANZAC Day	April 25
Queen's Birthday	Early June
Christmas Day	December 25
Boxing Day	December 26

Timeline

Australian History

Humans start migrating to Australia. **ca. 40,000 –60,000 years ago**

Dutch sailor Willem Jansz is the first European to visit Australia.	1606
Dutch explorer Abel Tasman lands on Van Diemen's Land (now Tasmania).	1642
Captain James Cook claims eastern Australia for Britain.	1770
The First Fleet, carrying convicts and guards, arrives in Botany Bay.	1788
Colonists kill or force out all the Aborigines in Tasmania.	1828– 1832

World History

ca. 2500 BCE	Egyptians build the pyramids and the Sphinx in Giza.
ca. 563 BCE	The Buddha is born in India.
313 CE	The Roman emperor Constantine legalizes Christianity.
610	The Prophet Muhammad begins preaching a new religion called Islam.
1054	The Eastern (Orthodox) and Western (Roman Catholic) Churches break apart.
1095	The Crusades begin.
1215	King John seals the Magna Carta.
1300s	The Renaissance begins in Italy.
1347	The plague sweeps through Europe.
1453	Ottoman Turks capture Constantinople, conquering the Byzantine Empire.
1492	Columbus arrives in North America.
1500s	Reformers break away from the Catholic Church, and Protestantism is born.
1776	The U.S. Declaration of Independence is signed.
1789	The French Revolution begins.

Australian History		World History	
New constitutions make the Australian colonies more democratic.	1850s		
The Australian gold rush begins.	1851		
Afghan camel drivers first arrive in Australia.	1860		
The first anti-Chinese laws are passed, beginning the White Australia policy.	1861		
		1865	The American Civil War ends.
Britain stops sending convicts to Australia.	1868		
		1879	The first practical lightbulb is invented.
The Australian colonies join together to become a nation.	1901		
White women gain the right to vote in federal elections.	1902		
About 330,000 Australian troops fight in World War I.	1914–1918	1914	World War I begins.
		1917	The Bolshevik Revolution brings communism to Russia.
		1929	A worldwide economic depression begins.
		1939	World War II begins.
Australians repel the Japanese in the Battle for Australia during World War II.	1942	1945	World War II ends.
Australia begins inviting large numbers of European immigrants in.	Late 1940s		
Melbourne hosts the Summer Olympic Games.	1956	1957	The Vietnam War begins.
Aborigines are recognized by the amended constitution.	1967	1969	Humans land on the Moon.
The last parts of the White Australia policy are abandoned.	1973	1975	The Vietnam War ends.
		1989	The Berlin Wall is torn down as communism crumbles in Eastern Europe.
The Mabo decision gives indigenous Australians the right to claim title to some traditional land.	1992	1991	The Soviet Union breaks into separate states.
Australia issues a report apologizing for removing Aboriginal children from their mothers.	1997		
Sydney hosts the Summer Olympic Games.	2000	2001	Terrorists attack the World Trade Center in New York City and the Pentagon near Washington, D.C.
		2004	A tsunami in the Indian Ocean destroys coastlines in Africa, India, and Southeast Asia.
Julia Eileen Gillard becomes Australia's first female prime minister.	2010	2008	The United States elects its first African American president.

Fast Facts

Official name: Commonwealth of Australia

Capital: Canberra

Official language: None, but the national language is English

Brisbane

Australian flag

Official religion:	None
Year founded:	1901
National anthem:	"Advance Australia Fair"
Type of government:	Constitutional monarchy and parliamentary democracy
Head of state:	British monarch through the governor-general
Head of government:	Prime minister
Area:	2,973,952 square miles (7,702,500 sq km)
Latitude and longitude of geographic center:	25°37'S, 134°21'E
Highest elevation:	Mount Kosciuszko, 7,310 feet (2,228 m) above sea level
Lowest elevation:	Lake Eyre, 49 feet (15 m) below sea level
Longest river:	Darling, 1,702 miles (2,739 km) long
Highest temperature:	123.3°F (50.7°C) at Oodnadatta Airport, South Australia, on January 2, 1960
Lowest temperature:	−9.4°F (−23°C) at Kosciuszko Chalet, New South Wales, on June 29, 1994

Ninety Mile Beach

Sydney Opera House

Currency

National population:	22,743,461 (2011 est.)	
Population of largest cities (2011 est.):	Sydney	4,596,328
	Melbourne	4,092,430
	Brisbane	2,056,290
	Adelaide	1,206,899
	Perth	1,554,769

Famous landmarks:

- ▶ *Blue Mountains,* west of Sydney
- ▶ *Great Barrier Reef,* off Queensland
- ▶ *Sydney Harbour Bridge,* Sydney
- ▶ *Sydney Opera House,* Sydney
- ▶ *Uluru/Ayers Rock,* Northern Territory

Economy: The largest industry in Australia today is mining for export, primarily to China. Australia has the world's largest supplies of uranium, industrial diamonds, bauxite for aluminum, and coal, with huge deposits of iron ore. Australian sheep stations are the world's main producers of wool. Wheat and sugar are important crops both for use at home and for export. Cotton, hemp, wine grapes, and tobacco are also grown. The primary areas of manufacturing are beverages and processed foods; petroleum and coal products; metals; and machinery. Australia also manufactures cars.

Currency: The Australian dollar. In 2011, A$1 was worth about US$1.06.

System of weights and measures: Metric system

Literacy rate: 99%

College students

Hugh Jackman

Common Australian words and phrases:

barbie	barbecue
bloke	man
chalky	teacher
cobber	friend
crook	ill, or badly made
fair dinkum	genuine
fair go	an equal chance
g'day	hello, good day
never never	the outback
sparky	electrician
strewth!	gee whiz

Notable Australians:

Cate Blanchett (1969–)
Actor

Russell Crowe (1964–)
Actor

Dawn Fraser (1937–)
Swimmer

Hugh Jackman (1968–)
Actor

Rupert Murdoch (1931–)
Media executive

Keith Urban (1967–)
Singer/songwriter

Patrick White (1912–1990)
Winner of 1973 Nobel Prize in Literature

To Find Out More

Books

▶ Arnold, Caroline. *Uluru: Australia's Aboriginal Heart*. New York: Clarion Books, 2003.

▶ Cefrey, Holly. *Exploring Australia: Using Charts, Graphs, and Tables*. New York: PowerKids Press, 2004.

▶ Darian-Smith, Kate. *Australia, Antarctica, and the Pacific*. Milwaukee, WI: World Almanac Library, 2006.

▶ Kingston, W. H. G. *Adventures in Australia*. Fairfield, IA: 1st World Library-Literary Society, 2007.

▶ Lindsay, Norman. *The Magic Pudding*. New York: New York Review of Books, 2004.

▶ McPhee, Margaret. *Australia*. North Vancouver, BC, Canada: Whitecap Books, 2010.

▶ Rajendra, Vijeya, and Sundran Rajendra. *Australia*. New York: Marshall Cavendish, 2002.

DVDs

▶ *Australia*. 20th Century Fox, 2009.

▶ *Australia—Land Beyond Time*. Magic Play, 2004.

▶ *Australia Revealed*. Discovery Atlas. Discovery Channel, 2007.

Web Sites

▶ **Aussie Educator: A Total Education Page for Australia**
www.aussieeducator.org.au
/reference/general
/famousaustralians.html
To read biographies and see videos of famous Australians.

▶ **Chinese Museum**
www.chinesemuseum.com.au
Visit this Melbourne museum on the Web.

▶ **National Museum of Australia**
www.nma.gov.au
For many interactive stories.

▶ **100 Years—The Australian Story**
www.abc.net.au/100years
See transcripts of the text and video highlights of this ABC-TV documentary.

Organizations and Embassies

▶ **Australian High Commission**
Suite 710
50 O'Connor Street
Ottawa, Ontario K1P 6L2, Canada
613/236-0841
www.canada.embassy.gov.au

▶ **Embassy of Australia**
1601 Massachusetts Avenue, NW
Washington, DC 20036
202/797-3000
www.usa.embassy.gov.au/whwh
/home.html

▶ **Visit this Scholastic Web site for more information on Australia:**
www.factsfornow.scholastic.com

Index

Page numbers in *italics* indicate illustrations.

Meet the Author

Jean F. Blashfield delights in learning lots of fascinating things about places and the people who live in them. Sometimes she learns too much! She says that when writing a book for young people, she's as challenged by what to leave out of the book as what to put in. This is especially true for the book on Australia because so much of the country and its culture are like the United States, and yet so much is fascinatingly different.

She started out by reading Bill Bryson's book, *In a Sunburned Country.* He was able to travel to so many more places in Australia than Blashfield has been able to. Because of her research into contemporary Australia, she now has on her computer the music of some of the indigenous musicians.

Blashfield has written more than 160 books, most of them for young people. Many of them have been for the Enchantment of the World and America the Beautiful series published by Scholastic/Children's Press. Besides writing about interesting places, she also loves history and science. In fact, one of her advantages as a writer is that she becomes engaged by just about every subject she investigates. She has created an encyclopedia of aviation and space, written popular books on murderers and house plants, and had a lot of fun creating a book on the things women

have done, called *Hellraisers, Heroines, and Holy Women*. She also founded the Dungeons & Dragons fantasy book department, which is now part of Wizards of the Coast.

Born in Madison, Wisconsin, Jean Blashfield grew up in the Chicago area. She graduated from the University of Michigan and worked for publishers in Chicago and New York, and for NASA in Washington, D.C. She returned to Wisconsin and the Lake Geneva area when she married Wallace Black (a publisher, writer, and pilot) and began to raise a family. She has two grown children, one a medieval history professor and one a university administrator at Stanford. Each of them has presented her with grandchildren, whom she adores. They have taught her even more than she already knew. She treasures her cats and her computers, though not always in that order. She is an avid Internet surfer, but she'll never give up her trips to the library.

Photo Credits